The Privileged Addict

Charles A Peabody

Charles A Peabody Books

Copyright 2010. All rights reserved.

ISBN 978-0-615-48007-7

We are not human beings on a spiritual journey.

We are spiritual beings on a human journey.

-Pierre Teilhard de Chardin

CONTENTS

PREFACE

The active addict, or the sober yet untreated one, is a truly selfish being who harms nearly everything he comes into contact with. The ripple effect of his behavior is far reaching, as he gradually destroys all things precious in life. Decades seem to drift by with a constant need for more powerful and effective treatment for alcoholism and drug addiction. Why? Because the slew of historical and conventional treatment methods have often failed to effect lasting change in the addict, let alone enduring happiness. And while I have been desperate to address the need for a spiritual solution ever since I recovered, I must admit that I also love to write. Left with this predicament, I chose to write an informative memoir - the intense story of my descent into paralyzing depressions and chronic drug addiction, as well as the process I went through to recover and to develop a spiritual life that has brought untold miracles.

My own path of drug addiction and spiritual decay led me to a place where there was no use for doctors, social workers, psychiatrists or medications. The people who had a hand in saving my life were just a group of junkies. Recovered junkies. There was a glow within them that was unmistakable. It is one thing to achieve physical sobriety, but a whole other thing to become *recovered*. I'd never seen sober addicts who carried such strength, peace, wisdom, and a willingness to help others for nothing in return. I asked myself how were they so okay? Why weren't they struggling anymore? Why was it so simple for them to not just stay sober but also to handle other thoughts, feelings, and life problems? And for some reason the universe conspired to bring me to this place.

The staff up north pulled the 12 Steps of Alcoholics Anonymous out of AA's original textbook, known as the Big Book. What I never realized was that when the program of AA was conceived back in the 1930's, it had little to do with meetings, stories, coffee, or holding on by a thread "one day at a time". The 12 Steps are a rigorous set of actions based on certain moral and spiritual principles you'd find at the core of any religious tradition throughout time. For me, getting better required an internal overhaul. I can't simply remove my addiction. I must replace it with something as powerful as the addiction itself. And I discovered that by taking consistent right action, something quite mystical occurs.

One of my hopes is that this book will illuminate the flaws scattered throughout conventional treatment methods as well as the crucial ingredient necessary for lasting recovery, peace of mind, and a meaningful life. I also hope that you will start reading my story and be done in a few hours. I've made every effort to open myself up and tell my tale of crippling depressions, chronic drug use, social paralysis, identity crises, assaults, car accidents, lock-ups, and a trip to the mental hospital in four-point restraints. I have described the people who I have run over and abused repeatedly, the way I have shattered their spirits, and the things I have stolen from them. I have tried to take you along as a passenger through my journey into hell, stuck in hell, and back out for good.

The story ahead weaves back and forth, from my life as a train off the rails to the specific process I undertook to recover. My story intertwines with my education up north and you will see how I managed to fail repeatedly to get better over the course of my life. For an addict who is spiritually sick, people, places, pills, doctors or self-help gurus are completely useless. There is, however, one thing that *can* fix us, and it isn't of this earth. While I have no fundamentalist religious beliefs or follow any one doctrine strictly, I am sure of the power of something much greater than us. God, for sure, is a loaded word, and though I choose to use it to describe this great power, we must remember that it is simply a three-letter word meant to convey an idea. I have no doubt that it was God who changed me forever one night up north.

Some of my views on addiction and recovery are somewhat controversial. Let me say in advance that I mean no offense to any particular program or method of self-healing. We all have our own experiences, and many different things have worked for many different people. I, though, being a drug addict, needed a solution for drug addiction, and a solution I have found. There is a way to recover from addiction and depression for good. There is hope for all who suffer. The answer is quite simple, though not easy.

Finally, I am aware of recent scandals regarding the credibility of addiction memoirs. I am happy to report that what you are about to read is actually true. To authenticate my story, I have scattered actual documents throughout the book, including police reports, hospital notes, accident narratives, and several others. In fact, some of the initial feedback I got from those close to me implied that I held back a bit. I've since made some changes and now I'll let you be the judge. I hope you enjoy this wild ride of darkness, light, transformation, and miracles.

For Isabelle

INTRODUCTION

Sunny days were the worst... time moved like a slug. I was 18 years old and life was already reduced to constant agony. Especially those hot, steamy, summer days on the weekend when everything is lush and people are out driving around with friends, having fun, swimming, playing, laughing, and living. I'm not sure what they were doing, but I am sure they were enjoying life and I hated myself for it. I could feel it... I was missing out. I peeled myself out of bed and looked at my skinny body. The sight of it alone swallowed me back into a crippling depression. Getting drunk or high only made it worse. No appetite. No senses. No pleasure. No desire for anything. Couldn't even masturbate. What a waste.

Grey, cloudy, windy days were much easier. They allowed me to rationalize not doing anything at all, not that I did anything anyway. Overcast skies meant it was okay to do absolutely nothing for the world except remain completely dysfunctional. But when the ocean glistened, flowers showed blooms, wildlife buzzed, people made noise, and the gold color of the sun reflecting off the tree leaves looked so beautiful, all of it just compounded my awful feelings. The beauty of summer only reminded me of how empty I felt inside. A veil of darkness smothered every inch of experience as I entered some unique depths of depression. That's when I knew I was really screwed, when nothing in this world could mend my spirit, until...

1

JUNK MARATHON

Sitting in my unearned manager's office, I felt too lazy to walk about ten feet to the bathroom to break up lines of heroin and sniff them before dealing with my next set of clients. A father and mother sat outside my office on a grungy couch, waiting for me to find their little girl a nice apartment to begin her college career. I made them wait as I entertained the thought of sniffing the dope right off my desk. It was too fun to pass up. I pulled out a folded up piece of paper, unwrapped it, and let some of the brown powder slide onto my desk. Why not? They weren't looking. All I had to do was put it on a folder, open up a drawer, lay the folder across, bend over to make like I was grabbing something, and sniff away. What a cinch!

Pin-eyed and jammed out of my mind, I drove countless numbers of entrusting families around, concocting imaginative and often illegal lies designed to clothe rat-infested dumps in silk and pearls. I glowed inside when I saw their checks come out. I was 28 years old and the only thing that went through my mind was heroin. But it was getting a bit complicated.

I lost an OC 80 (OxyContin – 80 milligrams) in a colleague's car one day at the gym and drove back to his house to look for tools to extract a SINGLE PILL. I must have appeared to be a freelance mechanic, having entire pieces of his interior unscrewed and laid out over the sidewalk. For hours, I deconstructed and demolished the poor guy's Honda. So screw pills. We started buying grams of heroin everyday from a kid at Northeastern University.

My savings dwindled. I was looking skeletal. Sounds a bit deranged, but there was absolutely no doubt in my mind that I looked normal. I was 70 pounds underweight yet considered myself to be completely gorgeous. I went to the gym to pretend I was okay and to try to balance out the effects of the heroin before coming home to my wife. I think my favorite part of the gym experience was sniffing lines in the parking lot before working out. Actually, it's a toss up between either that or nodding off in the steam room. I guess I should mention that 'nodding off' occurs when you are *really* high on heroin and can be characterized by sweeping in and out of consciousness.

I tried all sorts of things to make myself look normal again. Some nights I elected to stuff as many cupcakes as I could down my throat in an effort to gain back some of the weight I'd lost. That didn't really work. It wasn't long before a colleague at work commented on how thin I was. I looked at him in astonishment.

"What the hell are you talking about, buddy? Look at me! I'm fucking huge. Bro, I've been going to the gym. Look at these guns. What, you can't see that?"

Somehow I didn't notice my rib cage pushing though the skin of my chest. I was 6', 2" and about 210 lbs when the run started. Soon I was down to 170, 160, 150, 140...

When Northeastern Kid was out of commission from one of his frequent, overdose-related seizures, I had to pick up OxyContin from a girl I knew in the suburbs. Since her parents worked the night shift, I had to get in and out before 7:00 a.m. Time to really start honing my bullshit. On those days, I woke up much earlier than usual. Easy. I could make it look to my wife like I'm being a good, responsible husband by getting to work early. The difficult part was not just getting over to Suburb Girl's house that early, but getting out before 7:00 a.m. If she wasn't up getting high, she was temporarily unconscious. Twenty phone calls successively didn't come close to rousing my fellow scumbag. So I'd wait in the hallway until she called my cell phone, and when it finally rang, that's when my heart rang with pure and unyielding happiness.

Inside her bedroom, I bought the OC 80s and immediately shaved one down to a fine powder and sniffed it. One big line in each nostril. Then I ate one. Then I sniffed another one, if my daily supply warranted. I took the rest to work with me. I cherished them and carefully stowed them away. Losing one was like a close friend dying… or worse.

Driving into Boston afterwards was always a production; joint in one hand, cigarette in the other, coffee spilling, and on the cell phone lying to a client as to why I was running late to our appointment. Somewhat out of character, I began running so late for landlord meetings and lease signings that I had to sniff lines of dope in the car while flying down the highway. That entailed speeding around 90 mph with a knee on the wheel and balancing a piece of paper on my lap so I could shave down the OxyContin with my sieve. You have to keep your knee on the wheel but pull up the paper and sniff it without looking down for too long.

Once the car was totaled, it was difficult to get Suburb Girl's house by 7:00 a.m. I had to wake up at painfully uncharacteristic times, walk downtown to catch the train from Manchester Center, take it a few stops to Beverly, call a cab, take the cab to Suburb Girl's house, run up, get the OxyContin, sniff one, run back down, take the cab back to the train station, and pick up the next train to Boston. To be honest, I usually felt so proud for pulling it all off that I treated myself to one more thick line of death on the packed morning train. I'd start coughing to give myself a reason to bend over, allowing me to rip lines off the train seat - right next to normal people who could actually go to work sober. Imagine that.

After relief saturated my brain and pulled me out of continual withdrawals, I began planning out the rest of my day. Planning the day was coming up with lies to feed to my boss, clients, colleagues, everyone. I could lie on the spot. I am a natural liar. I only spent time devising clever bullshit when it came to my poor wife, because if anyone couldn't find out about me, it was Wife.

When Suburb Girl and Northeastern Kid both ran out, I had to resort to Spanish Guy in Dorchester. Spanish Guy days had to be meticulously executed. He slept in, so I had to get up later and chat for a while with my sweetheart, which involved explaining why I weighed 140 pounds, why my pelvis and ribs were sticking out through my skin, and why my facial skin had a greenish/yellowish hue similar to jaundice.

"Uh... honey, so basically you have no idea how stressful and exhausting my job is, do you? I have to run around all day long freaking out, trying to rent enough apartments to keep things going. No wonder I look like this. I work myself into the ground, eat shitty food in the city, and then sleep for, like, four hours a night! How do you not *get that*?"

I spent some time touching up on my Spanish fundamentals out of consideration for my dope dealer who didn't speak a word of English except "Five min', five min', I comin', I comin'". Waiting for Spanish Guy was the story of my life. "Five min, I comin'" meant another 30 minutes to an hour. I met him all over the city of Boston - in the projects of Charlestown, outside Happy Market in Dorchester, on Washington St. in Roxbury, over in Somerville on some corner. When he finally showed up, I had to drive him somewhere else to get the dope and then succumb to the rides he demanded all over Boston. I sniffed a half-gram right away. I got to work around 11:00 a.m. Work starts at 8:00 a.m. My boss only kept me on as manager because of the deals I was cranking out.

The new hire at our office turned out to be as demented as I was, which was absolutely wonderful. Having a using-buddy always makes it easier to rationalize your behavior. This guy was something else. He'd just start shooting up in the middle of the office when no one was around. I was impressed by how little he gave a shit.

One day Spanish Guy never showed up. I waited drenched in sweat outside the Charlestown projects. I scurried around looking for drug addicts. People screamed at me through their windows to get the hell out of there. Hours later, I approached the most sickly, malnourished, toothless woman I could find. She was perfect. Mini-skirt up to her ass, no teeth, yellow skin, dirty fingers. I knew she could hook me up. When she came back with a 40-bag of heroin, she pulled it out of her mouth, dripping with saliva infected with God knows what. I hobbled to my car, sweating buckets and hunched over from my writhing gut, so dope sick I could barely move. I took the bag that I just obtained from the creature's mouth, opened it up, and sniffed the whole thing. I knew I shouldn't put the bag in my mouth but it had some brown powder on it, so I threw it in there and sucked on it for as long as I could taste the gasoline-like, tangy flavor of the light brown heroin. I loved it. Insanity.

Another day no one answered the phone, so a few of us got into a mystery cab at Dudley Station in Roxbury, which ironically sits across from a free needle exchange center. Mystery Cabs are a last resort - independent cabbies willing to drive around interrogating other deadbeats to get what you want for an extra tip. We jumped in and drove around Dorchester for two hours as our chauffeur pulled up next to various community members, asking them for junk. After no drive-by luck, he took our money, went into one of Boston's thriving subsidies, and reappeared 30 minutes later with a gram of dirty dope. I wasn't sick for a couple more hours. Willing to go to almost any lengths to use, yet hardly any lengths to get better.

Soon even heroin lost an edginess that I began to crave like an indulgent pig. I didn't feel alive unless I was somewhere between absurdly high and overdosed. The solution: mix cocaine with dope. That put me in kind of a bind, though, because my heart reacted a tad sensitively to cocaine or crack. I sniffed monster lines, sweated profusely, threw up, and felt my body pounding - sort of like my chest was caving in on itself. I often thought my heart might explode, and when it didn't, that's when I started sniffing more. By the end of it all, it was several grams of heroin and cocaine everyday. I purposely neglect to mention constant weed, cigarettes, and benzodiazepines like Xanax and Valium, because that stuff is like aspirin to people like me.

The schemes I devised to obtain money were by most standards sociopathic. I preferred items of emotional manipulation like asthma medicine, rent, car insurance... you know, survival-type things I could whine about losing if the people who loved me didn't cough up the doe. I told friends that I lost gambling debts and how thugs were out to kill me. Sure it was a nightmare for them, but to me it was a display of true brilliance.

I never shot up. For some reason I never pushed a hypodermic needle into my arm. Perhaps being married kept me from shooting drugs. If my wife noticed fresh track marks on my arm, it'd be over. Or maybe it was because sniffing drugs still worked. Maybe I was just a fucking wimp. But whatever the reason, it didn't matter. Once you become an addict, there is no 'worse than'. Once you cross that line, you are equally screwed. I don't care what anyone says about being "… just some suburban dope sniffer."

Next to bed at night, I often fell to my knees and said silently, *God, forgive me for this sin. Forgive me for what I'm doing to my wife… to myself.* But I saw myself as a victim and blamed Wife for expecting too much. How could she possibly expect me not to be a heroin addict? I slave for this family of TWO all day long, at least when I'm conscious. Sure some accounts were overdrawn and credit cards were maxed out on 29% APR cash advances, but how dare she make such horrendous accusations? So I started fights just so I could leave the house alone. I had more important dates to be kept with Spanish Guy, Northeastern Kid, and Suburb Girl.

I took one day off a week to keep up with the good husband act. In her soft and loving voice, Wife tried to spend some time with me. "Sweetheart, maybe we could go to the farm today, you know, get some cider and donuts. You could help me pick out some food. I love going to the farm with you. I love just hanging out with you."

"Oh Sweetie, I'd love to... it's just that I completely forgot I promised what's-his-name that we'd play golf today."

Golf was perfect. A round of golf bought me at least four hours, hours I needed if I had to wait around to pick up. Usually I had no intention of actually hitting a golf ball, but I thought she was on to me one day, so I played it out. Dressed up in Nantucket-red khakis, a collared shirt and golf shoes, I picked up my clubs and left the house. Reduced to bumming rides after totaling my car, Wife drove me to the course nearest Suburb Girl. No sooner was she driving away than I was making my way down the streets of Beverly, hauling a bag of golf clubs in my red pants, soaked in sweat and emaciated.

I made it to Suburb Girl's house fully drenched. Her mother answered the door, looked at me with the clubs, and almost laughed out loud. She knew. And she refused to wake up her

OxyContin/Methadone-dealing daughter who was all cuddled up in her crusty flannel blanket and passed out on her stained, bare mattress. She wasn't coming to the door to rescue me. My heart dropped to the floor. I left and walked a mile back to the golf course when suddenly a suspicious Wife drove in and spotted me walking down the driveway. It's called fast-talking; I told her I was still waiting for my friend and just went to the clubhouse to do something healthy like get a vegetable sandwich and bottled water for the course. By the way, they don't serve vegetable sandwiches at the golf course. And locally grown, organic produce is not a priority either, but hey, she didn't know that.

I believed with all my heart that NOBODY suffers quite like I do. Nobody feels depression like me. Somehow I am different than the rest of the world and therefore I deserve to free myself from this curse. I deserve to do everything in my power to feel better.

I stumbled into my real estate office, dope-sick and freezing cold in late July. I couldn't find the energy to figure out how to get high for the day. I walked into the bathroom, looked in the mirror and saw a great shadow behind my eyes. I wanted to turn away but couldn't. I had to see what I'd become. I was going to die like this. I stared myself down in the crooked little mirror of our filthy bathroom to see what I could come up with. No answers. My world shriveled up like a black hole and then crumbled right there before me. I saw nobody looking back at me in the broken mirror. I saw a dark and twisted hole of evil. I saw a phony. Steady clouds of torment rolled in with heavy rains of restlessness. A sense of impending doom took over my body. I was losing it, and fast. I suddenly felt like getting high again and tried to formulate a plan. Get my body to a hospital, detox quickly, leave, find some money, blow some heroin.

I finally told Wife that I was struggling with drugs and needed to admit myself to a detoxification unit. Her heart sank, shattered, and broke into pieces. The walls of craziness and despair closed in on her. She had already begun spiraling into her own severe depression. I found her in bed on bright sunny days, staring out blankly, frozen in a fetal position. She felt her dreams of our life together and her idea of control combusting before her eyes.

Why do you need to go around trashing yourself? Aren't I enough for you? Why do you love heroin more than me?

Mom did all the work. All I gave a shit about was finding a place that passed out good meds. Still today I have the list of demands I wrote down on scrap paper and handed to her. At the bottom it says, "Most Important! Comfort." How about the irony of demanding the very problem that brings addicts down and causes endless pain to others: Comfort.

Off I went to the detoxification program at a hospital outside of Boston. A typical mix of addicts, psychotics, and the suicidal. Needless to say, addicts are and should be the last people paid any attention to in an emergency room. Why should some selfish asshole go ahead of people who are sick or injured beyond their control? We do it to ourselves and we should wait.

Then the first of many miracles occurred. The intake nurse told me I couldn't smoke cigarettes inside the ward that I'd be locked in for several days. I went nuts and screamed like a moron. I looked at everyone like they were supposed to appease my nicotine crutch and let me out for one last butt. No response. They stared back, waiting for me to calm down. I looked at Wife and Mom.

"I'm leaving this shithole for a cigarette! Can't you people see how ridiculous this is? This is a total fucking outrage."

I mean who goes to a locked detoxification/psychiatric ward without chain-smoking cigarettes? I got the madman stare from Mom and Wife. I just dragged them through a ten-hour wait in an emergency room and there I was about to walk away for a cigarette. The kicker was that no re-entry would be granted if I left against medical advice.

Maybe their frothing at the mouth rage gave me some perspective because something powerful soon came over me as I calmed down and refrained from running outside to suck down one last butt. The nurse appreciated my decision and slapped a nicotine patch on my arm. Where the hell was she thirty minutes ago? Man, I loved cigarettes with all my heart.

I let my clothes drop to the floor and put on a hospital gown. Someone slapped another nicotine patch on my arm. I wanted to suck on it. An intake assistant asked me about two hundred questions for insurance approval. I could've raised a child in the time it took for them to give me some medication: Librium and some other useless drug. I stepped onto a scale in an examination room. It read 149 pounds. Quick reminder: I'm 6', 2" and normally weigh about 210.

The second I began to feel better was the second I set up a family meeting to discuss bailing out. It was only the end of day two in the detox ward and I sang to Wife about all the grandiose changes I was to make personally and professionally.

"Honey, everything's fine now. I'm going to make millions. I know this guy and I'm going to get out of that bunghole office and make big money. I'm ready to go. Maybe, like, one more day and then I'm golden."

"Charlie, You look like you just got run over by a truck. It's been less than three days."

"Yeah, I know. I'm good. I'm a machine!"

Bitter social worker lady sure knew how sick I was.

"There's a difference between detoxification and treatment, Charlie."

"Um yeah, I know. I just wanna' go to the beach for one last walk. I just wanna' go home and wash lettuce and make a salad with my wife."

"Wow Charlie, you sure are a good salesman. Guess what? The beach will be there when you get back."

I verbally assaulted her just to keep pace, except it was me who was the one standing there in a hospital gown in a locked ward. Mom picked up the mammoth binder of treatment centers and showed me the list. She spent hours putting it together. I couldn't care less. It wasn't some thoughtful effort to me. It was something preventing me from using the way I wanted to. But God works through other people. That's when Mom remembered what some addiction specialist told her about a spiritual "gem" up North. It had the shortest minimum stay. Two weeks. Sold.

But the guys up North didn't mess around. There was no acceptance without some ground rules and a personal phone call. They needed to hear it from me directly.

"Is this Charlie?"

"Um, yeah. I want the bed."

"Are you really three days sober?"

"Yup."

"Can you walk up a flight of stairs?"

"Yup."

"Fine. You have to get up here by 3:00 or we can't do it."

I had no idea how lucky I was to get the chance to go up there. No idea.

Wife and Mom picked me up the next day with boxers, t-shirts, and 40 packs of cigarettes. The endless needs an addict has still fills me with some disgust, although now I can step back and understand that he or she is just one very sick and insane individual. I left the hospital in the dust, ripping a nicotine patch off and chain-smoking all the way up North. I complained about this and that. I whined and moaned loudly. I'm annoying.

My life was a vicious cycle. To most it's mind-boggling. The cycle was as follows: Relapse and destroy everything - get sober and sink into depression - as depression subsides, regain false confidence - get a job, make money, repair relationships and trust - relapse and destroy everything - get sober and sink into depression...

Productive, huh?

I burned bridges and destroyed people. I burned up resources and I sucked everyone I cared about dry. That is what I did. I sucked everything out of you and then moved on to the next person. All I can say is that Wife and Mom have a love for me beyond concept.

Does the Blue Direct Work?

*) 5-Day Program (optional
2 extra Out-
patient days
for 7 total
would possibly
be ok.

Opiates oxycotin, Herein
- parased, vicoden

*) Most Important! (Comfert)
- comfert
- medication to help sleep @
night
- medication to have very
comfertable detoxification
periods.

EMERSON HOSPITAL
133 ORNAC
CONCORD, MA 01742

DISCHARGE SUMMARY

Medical Record #: ▮▮▮▮
Patient Name: PEABODY, CHARLES
Admission Date: 07/24/05
Discharge Date: 07/27/05
Physician: ▮▮▮▮▮▮▮ MD

AGE ON ADMISSION: 28, date of birth March 21, 1977

This 28 year old male living with his wife in Manchester,
Massachusetts was admitted through the emergency department for
detox from opiates. He states that he had not been involved
with drugs until a friend offered him Oxycontin to try when
they were playing golf about 2 years ago. Since then he has
been using off and on. He admits to infrequent use of cocaine
and marijuana as well. During this time he states he has
stopped for as long as a week, but then relapsed. Precipitant
appears to be that his wife told him she will no longer put up
with his drug use. Although he makes good money as a real
estate broker, his drug use has put them in financial
difficulty.

PAST HISTORY: The patient reports a head injury in a motor
vehicle accident at the age of 19. This occurred in a head on
collision with a drunk driver. He has been diagnosed with
complex partial seizure disorder although he denies that he
does have one. He attended Middlesex School, a boarding school,
for 3 years during high school, then transferred to a private
day school near his home on the North Shore for his senior
year. He has one previous hospitalization at McLean in 2002
where he was diagnosed with major depression and reports being
discharged on Depakote and Zyprexa. He states he did not follow
through with the medications because they slowed him down. He
has been seeing a therapist recently.

Medically he reports having asthma.

FAMILY AND SOCIAL HISTORY: He states that both paternal
grandparents were alcoholic, paternal grandfather was also
bipolar and committed suicide. Maternal grandmother is also
reported as having bipolar illness. Father is alcoholic,
suffered from a mood disorder and is now at the late stage of
dementia.

SUBSTANCE ABUSE: The patient denies using alcohol for 3 years,
but does admit to daily use of opiates, marijuana most days and
sporadic use of cocaine. He estimates his use of tobacco as a
half to three quarters of a pack daily.

MENTAL STATUS ON ADMISSION: The patient was alert, oriented and
readily tells of his abilities. He has a somewhat hypomanic
presentation. He describes artistic talents, they are not
currently utilized. He has no evidence of hallucinations,
delusions or paranoia. He was not suicidal. He acknowledged his
appetite and sleep were disturbed, but attributes that to his
drug use. There is no legal involvement.

---

cc:

HOSPITAL

DISCHARGE SUMMARY

Medical Record #: ▓▓▓
Patient Name: PEABODY, CHARLES
Admission Date: 07/24/05
Discharge Date: 07/27/05
Physician: ▓▓▓ MD

MEDICATIONS: He is on no medications and reports no medication allergies or adverse drug reactions.

He was seen in medical consultation by ▓▓▓ who found no acute medical problems requiring intervention nor contraindicating psychiatric treatment.

LABORATORY VALUES ON ADMISSION: Showed a white cell count of 7.2, hemoglobin 15.3, hematocrit 46.7, platelet count 392. Serum sodium 142, potassium 4.4, chloride 106, carbon dioxide 29, BUN 9, creatinine 0.9, blood glucose 120. UDA was positive for cannabinoids, cocaine and opiates. Blood alcohol level was 0 at 11:25 in the morning, just prior to admission.

HOSPITAL COURSE: The patient was admitted to the unit and placed on a Clonidine protocol for detox from opiates. He was seen in addictions consultation by ▓▓▓ of addictions service. He was accepted to ▓▓▓ which has a 2 week residential rehabilitation program. Interestingly his detox was quite mild which he attributes to having his last dose 24 hours prior to admission.

He was initially resistant to attending any rehabilitation program, inpatient or outpatient, but as noted above, he did change his mind. With these plans in place the patient was discharged.

MEDICATIONS AT DISCHARGE: Albuterol and Advair for his asthma.

AFTERCARE PLAN: He was to enter the ▓▓▓ for 2 weeks of residential rehab. Following discharge he will attend AA and begin counseling at ▓▓▓ with therapist, ▓▓▓ ▓▓▓.

DISCHARGE DIAGNOSES: Axis I: Polysubstance abuse.
Axis II: Rule out cyclothymic personality.
Axis III: Asthma.
Axis IV: Marital tension and financial concerns.
Axis V: 55.

PR/ms24531

MEDQ   D:09/12/05 T:09/13/05

MD

CC:

Age/Sex: 30 M
Unit #: 490037
Admitted: 07/24/05
Status: DIS IN

Attending:
Account #: 4724069
Location: NS
Room/Bed: 516.1

PEABODY, CHARLES

Emerson Hospital Nursing **I VE** - PCU Summary Report With Notes

Problem/Goal/Intervention Description							
Activity Type	Occurred Date	Time	by	Recorded Date	Time	by	Comment	Sts Documented Units	Directions Change	From

Activity Date: 07/24/05   **Time: 1746.**

70020   Belongings List, Complete/Update   C   .on admission & PRN   OE
Document   07/24/05 1746 CG2   07/24/05 1746 CG2
DOCUMENT ITEMS BROUGHT TO & FROM THE HOSPITAL ON ADMISSION & DURING PT'S STAY

Personal Items		Disposition		Assistive Devices		Disposition
Jewelry: ✓		patient		Glasses: N		
Watch: ✓		patient		Dentures: N		
Clothing: ✓		patient		Hearing aid: N		
Wallet/Purse: ✓		patient		Cane: N		
Money: ✓		patient		Crutches: N		
Credit cards: ✓				Walker: N		
Other: ✓				Other: N		

List Jewelry: RING
List clothing:
Describe other items: CASSETTE PLAYER WALK MAN WITH TAPES

Belongings moved from: Belongings moved to:

Comment:

Valuables to cashier/safe: N   Patient's signature:
Ed Status: 07/24/05 1746 CG2   07/24/05 1746 CG2   A --> C
Activity Date: 07/24/05   **Time: 1747**

Patient Notes: BH Counselor Notes
- Create   07/24/05 1747 CG2   07/24/05 1829 CG2
Abnormal? N   Confidential? N
Admission Note: Pt is a 28 year old, caucasian, married, male who presented
to the emergency department for depression and opiate detox. He reports I
prior psychiatric admission to McClean Hospital in 2002, where he was
apparently diagnosed with Major Depression. Since his D/C from McClean
Hospital, pt has not been medication compliant. He was prescribed Depakote
and Zyprexa. During intake, this writer questioned pt about his
non-medication compliance. He states "I don't like to take meds...they make
me feel slowed and unable to focus. He is agreeable to medication trials
while on North 5, but is not sure that he will take upon D/C." He states "I
think I need to deal with the pain I am feeling and not mask it with meds.
Wife supported him in this decision, but encouraged him to take medications
was difficult on this period of depression and detox. Past hospitalization
was the result of an altercation when mother came to house and when
police arrived, they called the police and obtained section 12 for pt to be
transported to hospital as a result pt was apparently committed to McClean
Hospital. History of being restrained at McClean Hospital.

He denies any history of detox hospitalization; however shares that he has
been drinking since 13, drugging since 16 and then realizing it was becoming
problematic at about age 19. His longest period of sobriety was about 6
months. He is currently abusing Marijuana, Heroin, Oxycontin, Percocet and

---

Problem/Goal/Intervention Description							
Activity Type	Occurred Date	Time	by	Recorded Date	Time	by	Comment	Sts Documented Units	Directions Change	From

Activity Date: 07/24/05   **Time: 1747 (continued)**

Patient Notes: BH Counselor Notes (continued)
Cocaine (occasionally). He denies any alcohol use for the last 3 years. He
reports having attended AA in the past with no real interest in
attending again; but will try NA. Pt's father has history of alcohol abuse.

Pt reports precipitating factors as father diagnosis with end stage
Dementia....only about 6 months to live, poor sleep, poor appetite, increase
in drug use which has effected relationship with wife; who he reports "liking
very much." Pt reports feeling depressed, anxious, in agony and worried all
the time. He expressed concern that staff was laughing at him when he was
talking about his need for a cigarette out at the nurses station. When in the
OT room completing assessment, pt asked again if staff were "out there
laughing" at him. Assured him that this was not the case. He seemed
reassured, and wife states pt tends to be "really sensitive" to such things.
He denies any paranoia, but as stated in Triage report...pt is with some
grandiose comments; about making a lot or money and his status in the
workplace; wanting staff to know that he is manager/broker of real estate
business. Pt sees therapist, Richard Pisano, and reports it as helpful,
however Triage Clinician states family is considering talking to pt about
switching to a new therapist, as there has not been much change during time pt
has been seeing him.

Mother reports that pt was in a head on collision (at age 19) that caused him
to suffer from Complex Partial Seizure Disorder, which is not currently
treated, as pt denies having such an illness. Pt has asthma which is
treated with Advair and Albuterol inhalers. Seizure pads placed on bed, pt
stated understanding...but continues to deny the need for such precaution.

When pt arrived on the floor, he was irate with knowing that he could not go
off the unit for smoking break. Staff, wife and mother were able to redirect
pt back to focussing on reason for admission. He eventually calmed and
focussed on admission. He signed necessary paperwork; with exception of
Valuables List. Staff will offer when pt wakens. He ate grinder that wife
brought in and fluids are being pushed. Pt was medicated by nurse; see
nursing admission note.

Vitals on admission: T: 99.2, P: 80, BP: 121/83, 02: 96

Height: 6'2"
Weight: 149 pounds; 30 pound weight loss since increase in addiction;
        he reports 8 pounds in 1 week; nutrition consult ordered
Note Type   Description
No Type   None

Activity Date: 07/24/05   **Time: 2000**

10002   Vital Signs/Pulse Ox, Measure   A   4X/DAY   OE
Document   07/24/05 2000 JV2   07/24/05 2047 JV2
         Temperature: Temperature Source:
         Pulse: 88   Pulse Source: Monitor
         Blood Pressure: 118/74   BP Source: Left Arm

35

2

GATES OF FREEDOM

After 15 years of chronic alcoholism, drug addiction, severe depression, and a long car ride of repressed concern in Mom's clunky old Jetta, we arrived up North. Mom might have been able to upgrade her vehicle had she not just shelled out over two grand for the initial rehab fees.

We stepped out and were calmly greeted by a drug addict. The guy touring us around the campus was an addict. The intake manager was an addict. Everyone running the place was an addict. No doctors, no nurses, no social workers, no pharmaceuticals, no DSM-IV, none of that bullshit. Just a bunch of recovered addicts who knew what the hell they were talking about.

It was strange and defied expectations. I stumbled around with a staffer. The guy was grounded, strong, solid as a rock. I couldn't believe it.

"You mean you're a…"

"Yes. I'm a heroin addict."

I wasn't sure if I believed him. It didn't seem possible given his current condition. A chronic intravenous heroin user standing before me, completely alright? How is this guy okay, let alone that he wants to help me for nothing in return? The staff floored me with qualities I only dreamed of having. Filled with peace, confidence, and strength of spirit, all of them were fully recovered. It was a look in their eyes. It was the internal clarity of being rooted. It was spirit. Or God. Same thing.

The treatment center was beautiful. As I passed through the front gate, a large boulder covered with wildlife lay immediately to the right. Dogs appeared and frolicked about, grabbing attention from guests and staff (they call patients 'guests' up North). Beyond the boulder, several cottages surround a healthy circle of grass. Passing through the circle of grass was a stone pathway leading up to a non-denominational chapel that edged the back of the campus and woodlands beyond. The outer boundaries of the circle were lined with tall wildflowers, seasonal shrubs, perennials and annuals. Many contributed to the garden's exceptional manicure as grounds were maintained constantly.

But forget about the physical appeal of this place. There was a feeling. Walking around my new home, people approached me like good friends. I mistook them for staff members before discovering they were roommates. And they were transforming before my eyes from insane, miserable, post-detox wrecks to glowing, serene, stable, free men and women. The place had this ability to sort of calm everybody down and temporarily vaporize life's problems. We were all shielded from the noisy world back home, as sick minds and melodrama were washed away by an intangible energy. What the hell was going on? Whatever it was, I needed it.

Then it hit me. I sat on a couch waiting to be admitted. Wife to the left, Mom to the right. I thought I might die as I was suddenly struck with a kind of fear I'd never felt before. There was an intensity to it. It sped through me, permeating every cell in my body. I was overcome and overwhelmed. Bursting into tears, I embraced my loyal victims like a lost child. Leveled by circumstances, my time had come. Change now or die.

I knew the necessity of doing tremendous work on myself and was all too aware of the great spiritual, mental, psychological, and even physical work required to live a sober life without sinking into a mind-blowing depression. But change of this kind required long-term and consistent effort. How the hell does one go about doing that? How does a stubborn asshole get off the train he's been riding for fifteen years?

During the intake meeting, my belligerent comments were met with silence. I wasn't used to people who could disempower bullshit like Aikido masters disengaging ignorant and aggressive opponents. I flashed my wedding ring and made some comment about not needing to be separated from the female guests. The guy looked up and stared at me for a moment way beyond my already reduced comfort level. Swiftly, the wise staff looked inside me and tore through my crap. It was impressive. What I didn't know yet was that the people who pissed me off the most were the ones with a hand in saving my life. Tell an addict what he wants to hear and you might as well sign his death warrant.

Immediately after intake, Wife and Mom left me with some clothes and about fifty packs of cigarettes, and that was that.

A monitor approached me the first night. I tried to force myself to feel something, to pretend like I was already changing. It was balmy and dark. A haze of cigarette smoke floated under the overhang of the main lodge. I sat on an old wooden table trying to write something special in the notebook staff had given me. The guy stared at me for a moment, piercing my shell.

"I feel like there's something spiritually fucked up with you. I don't know; it's something in your eyes. Something off, way off."

A thought went through my head: *Who the hell is this guy telling me anything, especially what's messed up with my eyes?* Then a second thought: *How does this shithead know that my spiritual condition is the root of my problem?*

Then I met another guy. A gregarious fellow who ran his own fitness center. He was tall, tan, fit, constantly working out, and... he was absolutely nuts. Couldn't sit still. Suffered from the *real* kind of manic (bipolar) depression, along with voices in the head, hallucinations, everything you don't want. Plus he'd fallen down the abysmal pit of crack addiction. He took the Steps prescribed in the Big Book of Alcoholics Anonymous and did his very best. One day I saw him emerge from the chapel looking utterly different. His skin was flush and his posture had changed. He stood up tall, walking slowly and at ease. Something about him was fundamentally different. He was at peace and glowing from within.

From then on, he quietly read the paper and sat still for hours. No more voices. No more hallucinations. No more fidgeting. Gone from a clinically insane mess to a man filled with God and restored to sanity. You could just tell. Right then and there, I decided to do anything the staff told me and to do it with every ounce of energy I had.

Here's the deal: the folks up North weren't interested in much. They didn't give a shit about what I knew, where I'd been, or what I'd done. They didn't care about what I thought or believed. They certainly didn't care about how I felt. They weren't interested in my personal problems or sob stories. Only relevant to them was what I was going to do now and where I was headed. There was no place for self anymore.

Furthermore, these guys couldn't care less about mainstream AA. Meetings, stories, raffles, coffee, cookies… all that stuff meant nothing to them. They adhered to the spiritual principles and original program of action of the Twelve Steps of Alcoholics Anonymous, as it's laid out in the AA textbook, the Big Book, published in 1939. That and that alone got them better. Their only job was to take me through Steps 1 – 7, and then send me on my way to continue with 8 – 12. That's it. Willingness to go to any lengths to get better was the only necessary ingredient.

The daily schedule up North was about as simple as the prescription for recovery. Only the former was easy. Mornings began with chores - trash, toilets, floors, bedrooms, kitchen and living areas.

Chores are good for addicts. They calm us down, get us out of our heads, keep us in the moment.

By 9:00 a.m., all knuckleheads were due in the main lodge for a daily reflection. Staff read passages urging us to live by spiritual principles. Spiritual principle = moral principle, so let's not confuse the word 'spiritual' for abstract, hippie fluff. In other words, grow up, act right, and help others. One by one, we had the opportunity to add our own bullshit to the discussion, and those who passed on participating with regularity no doubt heard about it at some point, usually in front of the entire community. I always spoke, and yes it annoyed everybody, especially the staff. I'm pretty sure they *still* don't like me, but hey... nobody's perfect, eh?

We sat around the living room of an old wooden lodge. Tall ceilings blanketed the room as sturdy beams passed through the air from end to end. Wide planked wooden floors were coated with a worn Persian rug. A large fireplace sat along the wall behind a brick ledge smothered with self-help recovery books. Proverbial wisdom lay carved into the walls and beams. It was warm and cozy. This was a good place. In fact, miracles occurred here. Miracles exist. I saw them.

With mid-morning came Big Book class - my favorite thing, by far. Each day, one of the recovered staff members took us through the Big Book, line by line, breaking down clear-cut directions on the 12 Step process. Listening to them deliver facts about physical addiction, the underlying spiritual illness and the psychology of the insane mind was fascinating. They knew exactly what they were talking about and exactly how to word it.

Next we had something called "Chapel", a twenty-minute meditation accompanied by music. Basically we just blasted one of those sad and melodic slow songs. Great, just what I needed... to melt away into a pool of sentiment. As Sarah McLachlan entered my head, a wave of guilt crashed within and flooded me with horrible memories of what I'd done to my wife. I couldn't handle it. I burst into tears.

"Hey, don't worry about it. You're just realizing what a piece of shit you are. Perfectly normal. The pain you feel is good for you. It'll help you become more honest."

Smart guy. He was right. Tears gave way to relief after shedding some emotional skin. I had to shed both reasonable and unreasonable guilt, neither being any too healthy. Up North, I was called on to become a shield against self-pity.

Guest groups and free time skewered the afternoons, and after warm, delicious dinners, we piled into vans and drove off to AA or NA meetings. The locals gave us mixed reviews. Having received our PhD level education on the history of AA and the 12 Steps, we had quickly become official Big Book thumpers, and we let everyone know it.

It was the second night up North. As a few misfits hung around the main lodge, an older guy, clearly toughened by life, thin as a rail with a mustache, graying hair and sandpaper skin, paced back and forth engaging us with his loud, raspy voice. "Why not try this God thing? Nothing else ever worked. I 'bin shootin' dope every day since 1972. If I leave here and relapse again, I'll fuckin' die!"

Good point. But being a genius and all, I had to chime in.

"Whoa, whoa, wait a minute, chief. Anything's possible if you put your mind to it… if you really *want* something. I could get sober if I *wanted* to."

"Charlie, buddy, you're in rehab right now. Did you, uh, forget?"

Another impressive observation, but screw him. On I went.

"No, no, guys. There's no such thing as being powerless over alcohol. It's my choice. If I'm powerless than I can't ever get better. You need power over something in order to conquer it. In fact, I can have power over anything!"

Laughs and muttered comments. Another guy shoved his Big Book in my face. "You have no control! Can't you read? It says it right there. You have an *allergy* to drugs and alcohol, and you have no power over the *mental obsession*. You don't have the 'choice' anymore, and you can't get it back by yourself. Wake up!"

The guys got tired of me pretty quick.

"Hey Charlie?"

It was a middle-aged, soft-spoken ex-state trooper who was sprawled out on a couch. He turned his head in my direction and pointed his finger at me.

"Yeah?"

"If you're still thinking the way you are right now, you just wasted your first two days here. And I hope for your sake that you don't waste the whole two weeks or however long you're here for."

I don't know what it was, but those two sentences hit me like a ton of bricks. My heart sank as my ego shattered into bits. It felt like a giant stomped on my head. He was right. I had an illness. Sure I can ace school, make money, and get the girls. Sure I have some talent and creativity. But drugs and alcohol had me by the balls. They beat me. Right then, I began to understand how warped my thinking was.

In fact, my thinking was ridiculous. When my asthma doctor told me to buy hypoallergenic pillows because down feathers incited my asthma, I went out and bought those suckers right away, threw out my old ones, and never used feather pillows again. If he had told me to stay away from peanuts because I'd go into anaphylactic shock and die from an asthma attack, you bet I'd never even come close. I refused to eat trans-fats and fast food, obsessively eating organic. I filtered my water and bought lunch at Whole Foods Market… but smoked a pack and a half of cigarettes everyday. I brushed my teeth twice a day and flossed every night, but dove into a pile of cocaine coming from God knows where. I did all sorts of healthy things but sniffed heroin all day long. It's so absurd.

What the hell is wrong with me, you ask?

The answer is quite simple: I'm crazy.

Once the ex-trooper smothered my pride, I was sick to my stomach. Saturated with grief, I fell silent over the next twenty-four hours. Hard to explain, but it's like I finally got underneath something. Had I never fully conceded having a permanently damaged body with no mental control, I would have never recovered. I can't simply read the 1st Step on a poster on the wall, or understand it intellectually, or talk about it in an AA meeting. Nope, that's useless. I must wholeheartedly believe it. I must feel it in my cells, in my gut, in my heart.

I thanked the trooper and called Wife. It may have been the first time since birth that I was honest.

"I'm sick honey. I know I've inflicted hell upon you. I have a disease and I gave it to myself… but I think these guys know how to get me better. I love you."

3

BIRTH OF A MONSTER

I went to a small private school, the liberal equivalent of other country club offshoots that bless the north shore of Massachusetts. Mom told Dad she'd leave him in the blink of an eye if he so much as inquired about membership to Myopia – an iniquitous haven of the north shore affluent where ego and self-worth are fed by exclusivity and the façade of identity and wealth. All nonsense to dear Mom, who strived to break free from the puppet strings of social class. She didn't have much interest in buzzing around in gigantic SUVs on some of the smoothest roads in the world. She also didn't get "harried" traveling from the waterfront, to the hunt club, to the beach club, and all the way back to the waterfront in a single day... unless maybe you add Starbucks to the itinerary.

So I wound up in the new bohemian private school, just as expensive, though covered with a veil of acceptance and authentic expression. Nine years of elementary school can be summed up by the surfacing of innate insecurity and shame, inflated by a constant barrage of insults and sarcasm by the hands of the cool kids.

Generational layers of depression most likely accounted for me being shy beyond words. I was the boy everybody made fun of, except for a few smart girls who appreciated my harmless approach and intense academic focus. Every year, the cool kid and his cronies ganged up on me and called me names. There was one guy in particular who always seemed to have snot running out of his nose. He enjoyed calling my father a dickweed and telling everyone I slept with Mommy. My last name "Peabody" wasn't such a blessing either, turning out to be a convenient source of shaming material. "Pees-on-his-body", "Charlie Puberty", "Charlie Pee-brain" etc. The kids were brutal and everyday I was completely miserable. I slogged through each hour of elementary school feeling self-conscious and terrified.

Fortunately, I was stronger and bigger than most of the boys in my class. I couldn't take it anymore during recess one day and finally conjured up the guts to punch the snot-ridden, leader of cruelty. People could see the mark on his face and though inflicting physical harm upon him felt incredible for about five seconds, it changed nothing. He threatened to have his dad call a lawyer and I almost went to pieces. After making any kind of mistake, I thought I'd be severely punished and publically humiliated. Never was, of course, I just always assumed that all people did with their lives was think about ME, Charlie Peabody.

In sixth grade, another symbol of coolness rose up. This fellow couldn't stop calling me a "poser" around the other kids. His cruelty was, of course, fueled and amplified by hearing laughs from the surrounding crowd.

Poser meant follower. He called me this for listening to the same rock albums, like Guns n' Roses' *Appetite for Destruction* and Metallica's *Master of Puppets*. Sure I was a walking identity crisis, but I honestly liked the music and so it infuriated me. Soon the night came when I was cornered at a sleepover and had nowhere to go as he stabbed me verbally, hour after hour. Terror pumped through my heart and down into my gut as I sat there and took it, frozen by the nauseating sound of everyone laughing and making fun of me. I wanted to beat the daylight out of him yet strangely enough craved his approval throughout the entire school year.

There were moments of relief… the first coming back in second grade when realizing I had a major crush on a pretty girl with long brown hair, big brown eyes, and smooth brown skin. Extra batches of dopamine rushed through my brain and I felt high for the first time in my life. By the time sixth and seventh grades rolled around, her tan legs sent me reeling. I was obsessed, but not so much with her as with trying to keep this euphoric feeling of physical pleasure going.

I wrapped thirty or forty toys I found in my bedroom at home and brought them to her in a huge box. It was Christmas time and everyone figured I'd brought in a present for each kid in the class. A random student grabbed one and I snatched it back, giving them all to the girl. The next day her parents made her give them back, and so she brought the entire box into school… gifts fully wrapped. The embarrassment was beyond excruciating.

I first kissed a girl on the lips in fifth grade. Absolute bliss. It was by far the most incredible moment of my life thus far. She came over to my house in Beverly, and as we walked around holding hands, I felt a rush of attraction gripping me. Just before our play-date was over, we lay next to each other underneath my bed covers. I knew it was about to happen. I closed my eyes and moved in closer and closer, and then… whoops! I hit her nose. Ashamed and sweating all over, I retreated and then went in again, this time landing a direct hit on the lips. Instant pleasure sped through my body. I wanted to touch her.

Sexual ecstasy from fantasizing about the girls in my classes dragged me through the later elementary years. The rest of the time, I can't remember feeling satisfied with anything. All in all, the long road from kindergarten through eighth grade was agonizing. Time moved slowly.

At home, I practiced Classical pieces on the piano. I couldn't wait for my lessons every week. My teacher was a short Greek woman with a lot of love and a lot of attitude. I memorized everything and proudly performed Beethoven and Chopin in local recitals. Mom played me cassette tapes of Handel's *Water Music* at night to help me drift off to sleep. Needless to say, I had to keep that information buried or the kids at school would've had a field day. I still love Classical music, but I don't have to hide it anymore.

On the weekends, I played tennis with Dad and built forts. Building forts was very satisfying - an intricate fortress with rooms and passages. I loved having a place of my own and being shielded from everyone and everything. I crawled around the passages I built and peered out, feeling invisible. Coming out into the daylight was like coming down from a high. I never wanted to leave. The inevitable end of my imaginations was something I truly hated. Forts, however, don't work when you're a grown man. Eventually, I had to learn how to hide while standing right in front of everybody.

When the forts no longer gave me pleasure, I hounded Dad to buy me a bee-bee gun. I got off on setting up G.I. Joe figures in the bushes and demolishing them, limb by limb. Then I usually felt sad afterwards and tried to fix their broken arms and legs. I cried about the broken figures and other things that weren't real, things of no worldly consequence. It was the same with the army of stuffed animals that I set up as a protective wall around the edge of my bed after Nanny, my grandmother, plopped my sister and I down in front of The Exorcist when I was about five or six. But I tortured them also, and then cried about it afterwards. Go figure.

My life began to take on a pattern of extremes: overwhelmingly sad or over-excited, clinically depressed or speeding around on a manic tirade, consuming everything and everyone.

But I plowed through these early years of anguish and had my older cousin to look up to. He could drive, so we bought fireworks just over the border in Seabrook, New Hampshire. We had Roman candle wars. Roman candles are basically long sticks that shoot out balls of fire. We pointed them outward and shot fireballs at each other. Good fun, unless you get hit. We blew up all kinds of stuff with fireworks and dared each other constantly. We built jumps and flew into the air on dirt bikes. We jumped off the roofs of our houses to see who could make it without breaking a leg. We attacked bees' nests with cans of Raid until we got stung repeatedly. We did everything a kid could do for a rush until we figured out how high we could get from drinking booze, smoking weed, eating acid and mushrooms.

We don't have any family traditions or rites of passage. And no one around here is religious, let alone spiritual. So me becoming a man involved stealing booze from Pa, my grandfather, at the age of thirteen. This developing ritual first took place on Pa's sailboat in Maine with my older cousin. Given my pathetic construction of self-esteem, I was easily coaxed into steeling Pa's cheap vodka. I threw my cousin up on a pedestal and viciously craved his approval. So I drank it. But it's not his fault. I suppose I don't need to mention the fact that booze doesn't crawl its way up my body and force its way down my throat.

Once we polished off Pa's vodka, out came the whiskey. I poured it down my throat. Two minutes later, I found the only reason I needed to continue living – total intoxication. In that moment, false idols appeared before me and saved me from this thing called human life. But what do they say about false idols? Shortly after my demented spiritual experience, I fell overboard while trying to lean over the railing to pee. Sinking into the black sea, my celestial feelings suddenly morphed into adolescent terror. Death flashed before my eyes as I was quickly yanked out of the freezing Maine water and cast into the dingy that we dragged behind Pa's sailboat.

Waking up on Pa's sailboat was an early occasion by necessity. Pa was up at 5:45 a.m. for a morning dip before firing up breakfast in the main cabin. Normally his guests awoke to the crackling sound of frying eggs and bacon. Not today. I woke late, late for Pa anyway. I found myself in a pool of vomit. My bunk, sleeping bag and pillow were smothered by fresh thirteen-year-old puke.

Despite the fact Pa wasn't too thrilled, by the end of the day I'd forgotten all about it. Like magic. The hangover and its splitting headache, the empty feeling in my gut, the taste of throw up in my mouth, the fallout from my grandfather - all of it disappeared. By sundown, I was ready to go again. Just like that.

And then some years down the road, I stopped wasting my time with booze and weed and began shaving down OxyContin with a sieve and snorting it. When that became too expensive and my personal limitations gradually expired, I just bought heroin. From Chopin preludes to sticky, brown dope… there's no telling what Mom's bright little boy would become. And there's no rhyme or reason to it. I had love and comfort, good genes and famous lineage, yet my favorite thing to do was to sniff lines of heroin in my car. Alone.

Putting a drug into my body was an irreversible event. Once it hit my bloodstream and rocketed to my brain, there was utterly no desire, no will, and no other self-means to stop. Trying to stop was like trying to torture myself. That is my truth.

4

WATERED DOWN AA

The first order of business up North was to turn my previous exposure to Alcoholics Anonymous upside down and then knock it flat on its face. But in yet another failed effort would soon emerge great hope. For me, AA had been nothing but a meeting room where I sit in a chair, listen to sob stories, drink lukewarm instant coffee, depend on others to keep me sober, and maybe run up at the end to get a sobriety chip while people clap. Perhaps I even raise my hand and tell a story of my own. But stories, sobriety chips, and Maxwell House didn't get me better. I didn't need a social club. I have plenty of friends and let me tell you, they can't keep me sober. I also didn't need to reward myself with a 30-day sobriety chip just because I stopped hurting people. What I needed was to change, and that doesn't always involve feeling good or patting myself on the back.

Before going on, let me just say that I mean no offense for my views on modern AA, but I would be doing readers a disservice by not honestly describing my personal experience.

The first AA meeting I ever went to in Boston did little but fuel my desire to get plastered. How could I forget it? Sitting in my Fenway apartment one night, depressed from having to work with a mere six-pack, I began to flip through the small pamphlet advertising meeting times and locations for regional groups. I should have scrutinized the meeting symbols a bit more (OS = Open Speaker, CD = Closed Discussion, NS = Non-Smoking, M = Men, W = Women etc.).

It was a cold and rainy night. Wind gusts ripped through Back Bay streets. At the time, this was a tremendous effort towards my recovery. I was so proud when I found the meeting and made my way up the stoop of the Arlington St. Church. Peering around for a quick scout, all I could see were men in leather. Heads turned, eyes glowing. Chairs were offered. I sat down and realized I was smack dab in the middle of a Men's Gay AA Meeting (M, G). A speaker on the verge of breakdown unloaded about his life, depression, bills, eviction, boyfriend, blah, blah, blah… I couldn't deal anymore. I left and walked into the Pour House Grill a few blocks away for a vodka tonic and a round of Golden Tee Golf.

Trying to avoid dismay, I walked into another meeting at the Berkeley School of Music - a Young Person's Meeting (YP). Nothing useful. More stories. While sinking deeper into a funk, I spotted a blue book lying on the speaker table. No one referred to it. No one opened it. No mention of it at all. I asked the treasurer if I could have it and was charged five dollars, which had already gone to the Pour House's bartender. They gave it to me anyway and it sat in my studio for the next two years serving as a coaster. If someone told me what was contained within that book, I wouldn't have wasted another five years killing myself and hurting people. But that didn't happen. Here's what they told me.

"Oh, you don't need that shit. It's just a bunch of stories. All you gotta' do is put the plug in the jug and just keep comin'."

Translation: keep holding on by a thread because no one here can actually help you.

Young people are great, aren't they? They get emotional and say things like, "Yeah, today was *really* tough. I almost didn't make it. My selfish, asshole roommate pissed me off so much that I almost needed to drink, but I didn't! I mean, my alcoholism isn't even my fault; it's my fuckin' genes, man... It's my Dad! I think I need anti-depressants."

There's a guy I know from the north shore who goes to AA meetings all day, everyday. He's one of those biker types, you know, with the bandana, leather black pants, tank top, and braided red hair down to his ass. He gets up at the end and says, "Meetings, meetings, meetings… Go to meetings until you're blue in the face, and when you can't take it anymore and you can't sit through another meeting… go to a meeting. Meetings, meetings, meetings…" I hope this guy doesn't have a family at home because going to meetings all day would, yup, take up the whole day. In my local groups, I learned that it was all about me. Up North, I learned it was all about others.

But I think the most baffling AA slogan is "Sit down, shut up, and wait for the miracle to happen". Okay, so I've tried waiting and guess what happens? I go get high. Plus, miracles don't zap me in the face while I'm sitting on my ass doing nothing. And why drag myself all the way to AA just to keep my mouth shut? I'm going nuts here. I'm the guy who needs to open his mouth to ask, "How do I get better?"

I met staunch resistance in local AA groups. I dropped bombs all over the place once I'd been educated Up North. Rarely was I called on to speak. And double dipping is especially frowned upon. After a downtown Beverly gathering, a seemingly docile young female speaker accosted me outside a meetinghouse known as the White Whale. Her once humble countenance deteriorated as her mouth opened. "What are you, a fuckin' idiot? I didn't call on you 'cause the guys here will beat the shit out of you for speaking twice!"

Sounds like a tremendous way to recover.

A day later at a Manchester gathering, I found the speaker-turned-stand-up-comic rather unamusing. It was more like amateur comedy hour than a forum about alcoholism, and I was the only guy not laughing. Returning from the cigarette break, I found my chair removed and facing backwards on a stage behind the speaker podium. Now that is a wildly effective way to help people recover!

His few no-nonsense words, I remember clear as day. "God's never done shit for me! God doesn't keep me from drinkin' like these stupid whackos who say God talks to them. No friggin' Big Book keeps me sober either! I'm sober 'cause I *choose* to stay sober."

Huh???

I'm not sure that's the kind of program I needed after fifteen years of chronic drug addiction.

So I confronted him afterwards and here's what he said. "Spiritual? Kid, you got it all wrong! You see, we have an alcohol problem. Not a moral problem, not a psychological problem, not a spiritual problem, no, no, no. We got ourselves a drinkin' problem. See here boy, I still lie, cheat, call my wife a bitch, get into fights and what have you. I'm still an asshole, just a sober asshole!"

Oh, *now* I get it. It's finally clear to me. So I can thrash my wife, lie to people, steal money, maybe even sink into a depression, and it's all good so long as I'm sober? Wait a second, then how do I stay clean without wanting to slit my wrists? If this is what twenty-five years of recovery looks like then someone please shoot me in the head.

So all those posters on which the Twelve Steps hang look pretty, and the nice, big print is easy to read, but they're not going to fix me just hanging there. I can't finish them in my head during the meeting and by the time it's over, boom! I'm done. I also can't take a Step a year or wait a year before starting them. It's not something that I read or study, but something that I *do*.

Watered-down versions of the Twelve Steps are now mainstream in AA and in many treatment programs. But I'd be dead right now if I had approached recovery this way. I can't wait a year to get better. I especially can't wait a year to *feel* better.

Know what does attract me? Being a free man. Being recovered. Having peace of mind and strength of spirit. Having the power to walk through my fear and pain. Having the hole inside me filled with Love. The weirdoes up North told me that I needed a Power other than myself to do that, and I saw this Power within them. I listened to them because they were filled to the brim with something that actually fixes broken minds and hearts.

5

WALKING IDENTITY CRISIS

Common around my end of the north shore is a thick fog of stuffy bullshit. To be anybody is determined by your name, where you went to school, and how many figures you can personally account for. Of course, behind this phony vapor, the hopelessness of vanity and weightlessness of self takes its toll. But there is no solution around here for the need to be seen as important and privileged, so it is protocol to apply to a list of prestigious, private boarding schools for one's high school career. Candidates may be assessed by three variables: wealth, lineage, or IQ. Either one will do for acceptance. But the whole thing can be summed up for a loss. Preparation for the world consisted of an exclusive handful of trust-babies, piled together in an isolated haven of superiority, and not to be let out until four years of self-worship was complete.

The boarding school I chose was perfect on the surface; stunning campus, old New England buildings, a couple hundred brats, and familial ties that satisfied my stock... but I chose the place because I got hammered with my tour guide. That was all the insight I needed. Unfortunately, other than a few bad apples, the place was altogether stifling. Maybe that's why our severely disgruntled college advisor decided to tie a rather large weight to his ankle and jump into the school pond.

"Bye Ma, Bye Dad."

"Bye sweetie."

I think Mom cried a little when they first left me at boarding school. I watched them drive away. As the car disappeared, recurring thoughts began to enter my mind and they didn't leave for fifteen years. Later that night, I scurried around introducing myself to older kids, hounding them for booze or weed. One guy said there would be plenty of time for that and I should therefore calm down. That sort of comment immediately panicked me and I continued my search until I found a guy willing to share a fifth of vodka that he had stowed away.

Many shots later, I found myself seeing double in the student recreation center and figured I'd better get back to my dorm room before check-in. I took the darkest route through the soccer fields so no one would spot the trail of puke I left as I stumbled across campus. I thought I was home free when I made it back to my room and passed out. I'm sure my dorm master wanted to buy the incoherent nonsense I fed him about food poisoning and nausea except that it took some rather consistent effort to rouse the new kid who was unconscious by 9 p.m. Passing out before lights out wasn't common procedure. Off with a bang!

If anything could stop a budding train wreck, it might be a bad trip. Having temporarily escaped from boarding school for some breathing room, a few of my friends and I took a train into Boston. The mushrooms I got were wet, juicy, potent. The kid who sold them to me was only clear about one thing. "Whatever you do, DON'T eat them all at once. It would be the equivalent of dropping, like, twenty hits of acid."

Wrong thing to tell a guy like me. Warn me not to use something excessively because of the effect it might have and the only message my brain fires back in response is, 'GO DO IT, NOW!' I ate every shaving of the quarter-ounce sack of fungus.

We figured the New England Aquarium was a good place to explore the bounds of the mind, but walking up the entranceway I knew something was wrong. I felt nauseous and began losing control in the darkened hallway that led us into the underwater world. Sea animals approached us from behind glass, kids ran around screaming. I really couldn't deal with the whole aquarium situation. So we left and wound up in a Sharper Image store at Faneuil Hall.

Suddenly, I felt one of those fancy contraptions poking into my back. My friend turned some kind of massage machine with gigantic knobs protruding outward to the blow-your-brains-out setting, jammed it into my back, and ran it up and down my spine. The recent acid I'd done at my older cousin's house just before starting high school came back to haunt me, and no sooner had I felt the machine than I began losing my sight. By the way, word has it that acid lingers in the spinal cord for quite a while. It was as if I'd stood up too quickly with a head rush and saw all sorts of colors flying around. The problem wasn't losing sight temporarily, but that it didn't return. Every muscle in my body went dead as I fell to the ground.

It was Saturday afternoon and the store was packed. My friends looked at me lying on the ground and observed the skin on my face turning solid green. I muttered that it was no joke and to get me out of the city. They picked me up, carried me outside, and laid me down on a stoop. Certain of imminent death, I figured Mom and Dad would scold me viciously while visiting me in the emergency room. But being the trooper that I am, I eventually regained sight and muscle control, only to find that my baseball was swirling around in front of me, taking bites at my face.

The point here isn't storytelling so much. Well, maybe a little. But the greater point is that most people would have this sort of experience and stop using drugs - forever. Not me. The moment I was physically able to get up, I left Faneuil Hall to settle down with a few bong hits, and then drank enough alcohol to fall asleep. Then I bought some more of those juicy mushrooms.

So I was the angry kid at boarding school. I walked around shooting my inherited death glares at everybody. I made friends with older kids who used drugs. I observed them in their habitats - top floor quads where no freshman were socially authorized to go.

Upper classmen loved to haze the freshman newbies. One especially annoying rich guy from Texas enjoyed grinding his fist into the Jewish kid across the hall from me. Go figure. Others got off on the phony external power felt by commanding freshman to prepare Ramen Noodles, bring them cold sodas, or answer phone calls. Hazing wasn't my thing. The first time an older student tried to haze me, I just told him to go fuck himself. Fortunately, I wasn't especially small or scrawny. Or maybe it was just that my anger was altogether frightening. People stayed away from me. They sensed how deranged I was.

I never understood my freshman classmates. They still hung car posters on their walls and talked about, well… actually, I don't know what the hell they talked about. All I knew was that I couldn't relate to any of my fourteen year-old peers one bit. No interest. I naturally got along with older kids who had that half real/half not real drug-induced maturity. It's not authentic maturity, of course, it's just pain building up inside at a faster and more profound rate. We can attribute this sort of premature pain to the false comforts of drug use and self-pity. Or maybe it's just narcissism.

I soon became the guy who brought half-pounds of weed to school, sold shy bags to my fellow freshman, and took orders for liquor runs. I dressed up my Korean friend in a suit and tie and sent him into the local package store. The poor guy was only seventeen but easily passed for thirty-seven. The anxiety of getting caught only amplified the high, which helped me continue breaking any rule I could think of.

Running out of pot was a frequent and awful occurrence. When that happened, I had to scrape pot resin from the bowl and stem of my bong… over and over and over. I'd light it, some would burn, and the rest just melted through the bowl screen back into the stem, so I had to keep scraping it out again and again because at least I got a little hit each time. Trust me, the hot lighter burning my skin was well worth the few minutes of being high. This may not sound like your ideal Sunday afternoon, but for me, normalcy and routine were just too boring.

"Anyone in here? Charlie?"

It was the dorm master entering my room. I happened to be perched behind a tapestry with a bong hit exploding in my lungs. How long could I hold it in? Boy, this is exciting.

"Hello? Charlie?"

As he left, I blew it out my exhaust fan and patted myself on the back for being so impressive. Soon the staff went out of their way to bust me. It was like a game to them. Who could bust Charlie Peabody first? On second thought, maybe it was just a game to me.

There was one morning in particular that cemented my feeling towards marijuana. It was some pot that I smoked before acting class. I thought I was fine because it didn't immediately kick in. Wrong. As I sat there trying to listen to my drama teacher, I remember slowly becoming higher than I'd ever been. Everything began throbbing and I sort of went deaf to the sounds of the room. I couldn't make out what people were saying and I really didn't care. I retreated into my own little world of pleasure and detachment.

Acting class didn't go so well but from that moment on, weed had a special place in my heart. I could not fairly describe my fantasy-like love for it. I had to have own supply. Always. I wasn't interested in having someone smoke me up. I needed my own. And as the years went by, I loved weed more than people. I loved the way it smelled, the way it looked, the way it burned. I began growing it. I sat there and studied it like it was a treasure to behold. By the time I left boarding school, it was the only thing I cared about.

One of the stranger things about my particular high school is how the "cool" kids were the ones who did theatre arts. Besides my obsession for approval, I only stepped up for my first audition after a beautiful girl shot me one of those loaded smiles and coaxed me up on stage. I got the role and acting soon became one of the four semi-thrills of my life besides performing music, using drugs, and having sex.

By the second half of my freshman year, I grew my hair long and joined a band. Classically trained on piano and adept with guitar, drums and bass, I spent most of my time smoking weed and playing music. I sat in my dorm room amidst multi-colored tapestries watching Disney's Fantasia while tripping on mushrooms and practicing guitar.

All I cared to do was get high and listen to the Grateful Dead. I was counting on blessing the youth as the next Jerry Garcia. That didn't happen... although Jerry did teach me how to solo.

The rest of the time: more death glares. My goal was for the whole school to know how pissed off I was. I needed to be seen that way to cope with a divided self and to avoid any embarrassment. Embarrassment was a feeling I couldn't handle at all. I thought it might actually kill me.

One day a friend warned me of faculty concern, but I honestly didn't have a clue about the way I affected others - another symptom of pathological self-absorption. The dean of academics told me students were leaving classrooms due to their intense discomfort with my presence. I wasn't too interested in her assessment. In fact, it fed my ego to be seen as a tough guy. Maybe that's because I'm actually a fucking wimp. But after her report, rest assured I proceeded to scrutinize every student in every class, accusing all who left for the bathroom and staring them down upon reentry to cause even greater discomfort. Decent guy, huh? I guess I thought that I had to protect myself from something. From what, though? From a few uncomfortable feelings? I'm telling you, drug addicts should suck their thumbs so people can identify them.

These new character traits crippled me socially, especially following romantic break-ups - loud, dramatic break-ups sprinkled with untimely outbursts of verbal abuse. One certainty in life for me was the inevitable and out of control spiral with girlfriends, triggered by a compulsion to get the last word of filth in before sending the poor girls off in misery. It wasn't in my new wiring not to look into the eyes of my lovers and make them feel as small, stupid, and worthless as shit in the gutter. It was either that or I just flat out told them that I'd rather chew tobacco, get high and play Nintendo as opposed to hang out and cuddle.

Two weeks was my average girlfriend period. Any longer was unbearable. I walked away from my victims leaving them baffled, heartbroken, enraged. Girls thought I was a monster, and the truth is that I hated that perception. But at boarding school most young ladies found me unapproachable, and this is how I avoided them to do what was far more important.

It didn't take long for my rage at boarding school to spiral out of control. It was the beginning of my junior year. I lived in a top floor quad - a cool kid zone. Passed out drunk on our couch, a belligerent roommate woke me up to accuse me of taking his cigarettes. I didn't have them. In fact, I never really stole anything. Too much of a coward. I stole by lying to people who trusted me.

My roommate eventually stopped bugging me about his cigarettes and left the room, but I couldn't let it go. His sarcasm burned me up inside. I got up, tracked him down, and punched him in the face, landing a good blow to his eye. It bled and bruised.

As I awoke the next morning, I felt a wave of fear rush over me. He promised me he wouldn't say anything, but that's not how it works at boarding school. Everyone knew. So I decided to withdraw from the place entirely just to avoid any uncomfortable repercussions of my roommate's damaged eye. That was my strategy - avoid anything uncomfortable at all costs, even if it meant hurting people, taking no responsibility for anything, or sniffing heroin all day long.

Unfortunately, leaving school prematurely landed me in an outpatient program at a psychiatric hospital outside of Boston. Totally useless. Surrounded by suicidal girls, schizoid boys, and a few epileptics, I sat in group therapy as an angry kid who loved pot while the girl to my right slipped into a grand mal seizure and the girl to my left began gouging overgrown nails into her wrists. I knew this kind of treatment was a farce. I had no desire to stop using. I knew what I wanted to do. I wanted to get high... forever.

After drifting through the psychiatric program, I enrolled in a private day school in the north shore. Beverly public school wouldn't do for the Peabody boy, though I toured some of the bland halls and considered it on the basis that I could use drugs all day long and get away with murder. But that wasn't necessary. I was smart enough to do that at a small and scrutinizing private school. Even better, the school was a joke - a country club fairytale for rich kids who either didn't want to leave home or didn't get accepted into the more academically challenging boarding schools. I took four exams to account for the entire fall semester that I'd missed and slipped in relatively unnoticed. But eventually my reputation and long hair trailed me, and again both faculty and image-infirm principal began searching for ways to expel me. My answer was to graduate with honors and a head full of dreadlocks.

I wasn't so lucky with my thoughts and feelings. Something happened. It was a crush on a pretty girl that ignited the rapid downward spiral. As I approached her in the cafeteria one day, I suddenly became paralyzed by self-consciousness. I tried to be amusing and gregarious, but it quickly went from bad to worse. You know it's not good when you are aware of the words coming out of your mouth.

Then you begin the scathing internal analysis of all the idiotic stuff you just said.

Insecurity followed me home that afternoon and as the day wore on, I became increasingly crippled by depression. And it all happened so fast. I tried making some soup and couldn't even taste it. Whatever it was, it was growing in power every moment. All I could do was watch myself going clinical. I was eighteen years old.

The next few weeks in school, I felt self-conscious every second. Socializing made it worse. Much worse. Once the school year ended, I became completely dysfunctional. No energy. No appetite. No senses. No sexual desire. No anything desire. Paralyzed. I lay down at night and thoughts ripped through my mind, racy and speedy. I stopped spending time with anyone.

I decided the summer heat was the force that triggered the whole thing, and so I lived out a self-fulfilling prophecy every summer for the next few years, slipping into a depression every spring and lasting for months until early fall. The crisp weather seemed to pull me out of my funk, as I returned to some reduced productivity until the following spring.

After graduating high school in the midst of an emotional paralysis, I immediately ran away to Central Oregon to complete an

Outward Bound course. I figured some whitewater rafting and a bunch of self-help books on non-resistance, Zen meditation and the wisdom of the *Tao Te Ching* would prepare me for the University of Vermont. Instead, I moved up to North Hero, Vermont with some high school friends who had since become white, affluent Rastafarians... and no, I'm not kidding. Our plan was to start a reggae band.

However, living in the beautiful woods of Central Oregon for a few weeks provided a glimpse of what internal freedom felt like. Removing myself from the world cleared out my overactive head, stomped out the funk I was in, and put me back on the right track for a few days. I saw the secret to life in nature - the way it lets whatever comes come, and whatever goes go. It doesn't fight or resist what is happening. Why couldn't I just stop thinking altogether and do what nature does? But even though it cleansed my spirit and carried with it this wisdom, nature alone wasn't powerful enough to change the entire course of my life. Nature cannot make an insane addict sane again, especially when his friends have told him that Haile Selassie was the second coming of Christ and instructed him to play reggae music to the people.

Convinced I had now discovered the truth, I spun an entire identity out of ego and self-righteousness. I knew in my heart that I was supposed to become a freedom-fighting Rastafarian. I let my hair further devolve into a rat's nest during Outward Bound and spent a good deal of time shaping it back into dreadlocks before blessing the Green Mountains with my presence. I packed up my Dad-bought Volvo and plastered it with bumper stickers protesting social injustice, environmental degradation, and of course, Jah Rastafari stickers.

I passed an army vehicle on Rt. 89 and slowed down in front of it so army guy could stew over my bumper stickers, certain massive guilt would erupt inside him. I was out for pride and power, to teach the world lessons, to change people, to free army guy on Rt. 89 from his social ignorance. I'd change the entire course of his life by blasting reggae music and shaking my head around wildly as pot smoke wafted out of my car. Ah, yeah, okay.

I barely knew the fellow man-child I was renting a house with. The kids I attached myself to during my second high school were only important to me as user-friendly acquaintances. By the end of our senior year, we'd all pretty much lost our minds. White boys from the north shore of Massachusetts, one of the richest places in the entire world, suddenly decided we were victims of the evil Babylon system and were now bound together by our righteousness and superior belief in the divinity of Emperor Selassie, the former and last king of Ethiopia.

So there you have it. I was fairly certain that peace-loving Buddhist monks weren't all going straight to hell, but Christian fundamentalism fueled our so-called divine justification to smoke pot out of a coconut all day and deflect our pain and self-loathing onto the "satanic" principles of capitalism and colonialism. We cloaked ourselves with a phony countenance of love. We wrote songs and played reggae music as if we were sent to enlighten the world, saving lost souls who weren't blessed with our divine knowledge. God only knows what our poor folks thought.

And don't get me wrong, I love reggae music, but to claim it is God's will for us to bring Jah's message to the people and smoke pot out of a chalice because it's humbling... well, that's just useless to argue against.

The truth is that I was totally insane, living in North Hero to play reggae by night and spending my days walking around the city of Burlington, flashing my dreadlocks in an Adidas jump suit, trying to exude spiritual prowess in a wealthy New England college town. I suppose this is what happens when a privileged addict is left to his own devices. Or perhaps privileged idiot is more accurate.

Despite all this nonsense, by the time spring semester rolled around it became necessary to procure a job and take some classes at UVM in order to appease my poor family. The only gig I pursued was delivering bread at 3:00 in the morning. Driving around during off hours would allow me to get high before the day even started. But smoking weed after two to three hours of sleep and driving a bread truck around rural Vermont is not the best idea I ever had.

By the third day, I forgot to latch the back door of my little bread wagon. Taking the corner at a busy intersection is something I'll never forget. Hitting somewhere between 30 to 40 mph, the door swung open for every bread crate to go flying out of the back of my truck. There I was, praying for the traffic light to stay red, running back and forth from the sidewalk to the street, dreadlocks flying, picking up bread, carrying it back to safety, and throwing it in a pile on the sidewalk. I was so proud of myself for getting every piece of mangled baguettes and rolls off the road just as the light turned and cars began steaming towards me... and totally shocked to find out later that I hadn't been penciled in on the next day's shift.

Between reggae, worshipping King Selassie, and destroying bread, a girl found me. The revolving door of my heart swung open as I welcomed her (and a few other personalities) in.

I believe the people we attract to us are indeed those who, in a sense, mirror who and what we are at the time. On a superficial level, crossing paths with an angry driver reflects anger in myself. On a profound level, crossing paths with the chemicals of a lover and burning a diseased relationship to its end reflects the time, place and need to learn a life lesson. Mine? Not to enter the dangerous waters and shattered world of borderline personality disorder.

Led by my heart and truly a sucker, I fell into the intoxicating delusion of sex-love. She was tall and attractive with long, auburn hair. She invited me in and showered me with sex. We were melodramatic and wild. We held each other as if the stars conspired to bring us together, gazing into each others' eyes with emotion fueled by nothing but lust… and then after moments of pure fantasy, we'd rip each other apart with our words before further regressing into threatened primates. From normal to violent to victim and back again goes the borderline merry-go-round. What happens is you don't really break anyone's heart but your own.

I spiraled into another blistering depression. Every ounce of time and energy went to the girls I fell for. Intimacy pulled me so far away from myself that chemical imbalance was practically inevitable. Despite several failed attempts to send her back home for the summer break, she followed me back to Massachusetts, promising to rent her own apartment. Even Dad was somewhat confused when she refused to leave the house and repeatedly smashed his stone wall with her hippie truck. That's when I finally outsmarted her and staged a visit to her own incestuous world down south. My plan was to leave single-handed, and after just a few days I made it out unscathed... or so I thought.

Resting comfortably on a summer funk after the exodus of my southern beauty, I managed to hook up with some friends for a concert at the House of Blues in Cambridge, Massachusetts. We saw the Itals, an old, roots reggae band. The concert was hazy, claustrophobic, dreamlike. I tried to force myself to have a good time and feel thankful but couldn't ignore the sharp, suffocating combination of the smoke-filled room and the pressure I exerted on myself to act cool and calm in front of my friends.

The last thing I remember after leaving the concert was pulling up to a red light in Somerville. Some guy drove up next to us and rolled down his window.

"Hey, how-ah-ya'? Whatta' you guys up to?"

"We just saw a reggae show."

"That's cool. Anyone wanna' fight for money?"

We laughed at him and sped off…

I woke up two and a half days later with no recollection of what happened and no idea where I was. Couldn't move an inch of my body. Eyes still sealed shut from the operation. Two thoughts went through my head: *Something happened… I'm really fucked up* and *God help me.* Suddenly I heard a question.

"Charlie, can you move your right and left toes for me?"

They moved.

"Charlie, can you now move your right and left hands for me?"

Shouts of joy and relief came from outside the plastic bubble I lay paralyzed in. I heard Mom screaming. I'd passed the initial vegetable test.

Three friends and I were hit head-on by a drunk driver speeding the wrong way down Rt. 128, a local highway. Appearing suddenly, he hit us at the top of an incline as we both cruised at speeds of around 70 mph. When Mom realized he was lying next to me in the intensive care unit, she almost assaulted him. Didn't matter. He soon died from liver failure. We discovered he was a fellow north shore local driving his mother's car around with recently served divorce papers in the passenger seat. Typical Masshole.

I moved to a room two days after the ICU and left the hospital in less than a week. Eager to leave, I inquired about the protocol for discharge approval. Told I had to a) walk down the hall and back without fainting and b) pass a movement, I got up unassisted and immediately lost my balance. Flailing backwards and backpedaling in an effort to right myself, tubes from my wrists, arms, neck, nose, and of course, the catheter, all gradually began stretching and stretching until... snap! Every single tube flung out as I barreled against the wall across the hallway with a stream of piss trailing behind me. Maybe not the preferred method, but certainly one way to get the catheter out.

When that whole production was over, I got up a second time, walked down the hall and back, took a dump, and checked myself out.

My friends weren't so lucky. My buddy driving was found with his face implanted into the steering wheel and multiple broken bones, including an arm bone that had pushed right out through his skin. We were hit so hard that the engine was smashed through the dashboard, crushing the driver and my best childhood friend in the passenger seat. His ankle was destroyed and eventually fused together after countless surgeries. The impact flung me a good way from the back seat to the front. It collapsed a lung, knocked me unconscious with a major concussion, tore my spleen to shreds, and left multiple lacerations. My other friend in the backseat was the only one unharmed and fully conscious. All he saw and heard was death, whether it was the gurgling sounds coming from my mouth or our unconscious friend mashed into the steering wheel. The smell of blood and burnt rubber was for him to somehow assimilate.

A breathing tube was forced down my throat before pulling me from the car because I was stuck and getting critically insufficient oxygen levels for nearly half an hour, not to mention the lethal blood pressure levels from hemorrhaging so long.

On the dark highway in the dead of night, we were cut out of the small, two-door '86 Saab with the Jaws of Life. The driver and I were airlifted to the hospital and slowly brought back to life. The whole scene was lonely and terrorizing. But we survived out there for over thirty minutes without breathing machines and blood transfusions. Mom said God was busy and sent angels down to protect us. I don't know who was busy and who wasn't, but I know there was a Power present with us that night. Some thread or essence of love kept us alive. It is the same power that makes us move and do the things we do. It is the same reason that walls cannot build walls and I cannot build another me. It is something that flows through the air. Perhaps you can feel it?

There is a point, however, to be taken from this accident business. When normal people are nearly destroyed by a drunk driver barreling down the wrong way of the highway, they tend to commit immediately to lifelong seatbelt usage and total abstinence from drunk driving. They do this out of fear alone. Normal people experience serious accidents, medical warnings, the death of someone close, or the threats of an angry spouse and they stop drinking or using drugs for good. Just like that.

But me? A few months later, I was plastered behind the wheel and speeding around with no seatbelt. Sure I knew it was wrong, sure I knew that I had a rather significant problem, but I didn't care. It's called a warped mind. That's the thing about addiction. I lose everything and go get high anyway. I'm broken.

Anyhow, survival euphoria following the head-on collision of 1996 propelled me onto a pink cloud. I returned to the University of Vermont three weeks after surgery, enrolled in six classes, did my homework every night like a good boy, and even performed standing meditation for an hour, twice a week. I was heading for another 4.00 GPA and imagined myself as some kind of hero. But a year and a half of my Rastafarian repression finally took its toll as personal restraint reached its saturation point.

Crawling out of a box of religiosity, I relapsed and scorched the city of Burlington with my newly shaved head and some very loud and aggressive behavior. From meditation, homework, and praising Jah, to keg parties, sex fests, and mouthing off like a crazy baldhead. The crunchy community didn't react too well to my new look. But the truth is that I was in some trouble. I'd been jumped three times in Burlington, once by a local Vermont goon, and then twice more by entire groups of angry college kids after making passes at their girlfriends.

My potential for physical disaster alone necessitated a hasty exodus from UVM. So I moved back home with Dad. It was perfect. I drank more steadily against little opposition. Two untreated drunks living under a roof with no rules and no one who cared to clean up. Mom finally had it and moved into the People's Republic of Cambridge. But both of my parents were a bit confused.

"What are you going to do with yourself now that you've destroyed your semester at UVM and have left with no plans whatsoever?"

Good question.

I woke up hammered one morning after my 20th birthday and realized that I was late for some therapy appointment in Boston. Pissed off and stuck in the suburbs after blacking out, I was lucky to wake up on an old friend's couch, which helped me identify what town I was in. No car, no money. I began running down a busy street when some guy in a brand new Jeep Grand Cherokee rolled down his window and offered me a ride to the train. As I ran around the back of his car to the passenger side, he flung the door open and I ran smack into the corner of the metal door. It sailed through my eyelid. Blood gushed all over the car. I closed my eye and could see right through the lid. That can't be good.

The nurse at the emergency room asked me if I'd been drinking, what year it was, and who the president was. Such absurd and stupid questions infuriated me beyond words. Just the bitch look on her face singed my pride, and anyone who gave *Charles Augustus Peabody III* a hard time was going to have it. I formulated the cruelest insults and rehearsed them internally before ripping into her. So after one too many comments regarding her developmental challenges, I was transferred to Mass. Eye & Ear in Boston.

A few stitches and bare minimum sobriety later, I sat up in bed at Dad's house when a great sadness welled up from within. With increasing frequency, random moments of grief and despair overcame me. I couldn't ignore how wrong and terrible my current path was. I was strapped into a train of destruction, spiritual doom, and perpetual torment. I was all too aware of the change I needed to create but it felt like too enormous a mountain to climb. So I resorted to anger. Unfortunately, Mom and Sis were visiting. They wanted to make sure I was okay after my drunken eye surgery.

Nothing specifically set me off that night. Perhaps it was some childish frustration of not feeling listened to, not being heard, not being the center of attention. I flew out of bed and filled the powerless hole inside me with unbounded rage. I started wrecking my parents' house furiously. The sound of an insane person wrecking the house you are in is something you will never forget. I threw the TV around, smashed furniture to bits, destroyed all sorts of valuable stuff, dented walls and floors, and grilled my poor family with my demented death glares. Imagine that.

Thank God Sis was obsessed with mindless TV shows like 'Cops' and 'Rescue 911'. She fantasized about calling 911 and this was her chance. It's a good thing, too, because I couldn't care less about what I was doing.

Knowledge of the police arriving did little but spark a frantic initiative to grab my bag of weed before a slew of armed civil servants poured into our house. My derangement landed me with a well-deserved arrest and subsequent assault and battery charge. Add to that possession of a class D substance, but all dismissed by successfully manipulating my parents to spend thousands of hard-earned cash for a smooth talking lawyer. I'm surprised my attitude of entitlement didn't piss the Judge off more. It would have disgusted me. But a child remains a child until he changes, and so my good parents bailed me out a day later. I glared at them, walked away to my dealer's house, immediately started drinking, and begin ripping their hearts out all over again.

Oh, I also shunned my sister for about a year because she called the cops on me. I mean, how dare she interrupt me while I'm wrecking the house and terrorizing my family.

OPERATIVE REPORT

PEABODY, CHARLES A   From 07/01/1996 through 08/31/1996
MRN: ███████   Sex: M DOB: 3/21/1977   Age: 32y

7/30/1996   Accession # 38656   Unsigned

OPERATIVE REPORT

    NAME: PEABODY, CHARLES A   UNIT NO: 349-02-05

    DATE: 07/30/96   FLOOR:

    SURGEON: ████████

    ASST: ██████████ ████████████

    PREOPERATIVE DIAGNOSIS: STATUS POST TRAUMA, HYPOTENSION, GROSSLY
    POSITIVE PERITONEAL LAVAGE.

    POSTOPERATIVE DIAGNOSIS: MULTIPLE SPLENIC LACERATIONS

    NAME OF OPERATION: EXPLORATORY LAPAROTOMY, SPLENECTOMY, SUTURING OF
    FACIAL AND LEG LACERATIONS, FLEXIBLE BRONCHOSCOPY

    ANESTHESIA: General endotracheal anesthesia

    INDICATIONS FOR PROCEDURE: Briefly this is a 19-year-old man who was the
    back seat unrestrained passenger in a high speed motor vehicle accident.
    On the scene he was intubated for depressed mental status and was brought
    to the   Hospital Emergency Room with a blood pressure
    of 80/palp. Although he responded to volume he continued to drop his blood
    pressure into the 80's despite four liters of crystalloid resuscitation. A
    diagnostic peritoneal lavage revealed gross blood.   On his way to the
    operating room he obtained a head computerized tomography scan which
    revealed no surgical bleeding in the head.

    DESCRIPTION OF PROCEDURE: The patient was brought to the operating room
    and placed supine on the operating table. General endotracheal anesthesia
    was administered. The patient's neck, chest, abdomen and thighs were
    prepped and draped in the usual sterile fashion.   A midline incision was
    used to enter the abdominal peritoneal cavity and upon entrance to the
    peritoneal cavity a large amount of blood was noted.   The four quadrants
    were expeditiously packed in the usual fashion. Allowing the
    anesthesiologist to catch up with volume resuscitation the packs were
    gradually removed sequentially. There was no bleeding in the left or right
    lower quadrant.   There was no bleeding in the right upper quadrant.   There
    was massive bleeding emanating from the region of thespleen.   The spleen
    was delivered into the wound after the lienorenal and lienodiaphragmatic
    attachments were taken sharply and then bluntly.   The spleen was noted to
    be fractured in multiple sites with multiple avulsion injuries (grade 4
    injury).   The hilum was clamped with snaps taking great care to avoid the
    tail of the pancreas and the splenic vessels were suture ligated.   The left
    upper quadrant was then packed and the abdomen was explored in a careful
    fashion. Findings included no evidence of bowel injury, a small right iliac
    hematoma which was not expanding, small left renal hematoma that was not
    expanding, and no other evidence of surgery aside from that of the spleen.
    The left upper quadrant was once again checked for bleeding and meticulous
    hemostasis was obtained. A #8 French Jackson-Pratt drain was left in the

---

94

OPERATIVE REPORT (cont) from 07/01/1996 through 08/31/1996

PEABODY, CHARLES A

MRN: ████████   Sex: M   DOB: 3/21/1977   Age: 32y

splenic fossa.   The abdomen was closed with #1 PDS running sutures.   The wound was irrigated and then closed with staples. Attention was then drawn to the left thigh which had a small laceration after meticulous washout was closed. The Oral Surgery Service then came and sutured a deep laceration of the forehead. This will be dictated under separate cover. Next due to some blood in the endotracheal tube a flexible bronchoscopy was performed. The carina was visualized. There was some clot in the mid bronchi which was suctioned out. There was no evidence of acute injury. The patient tolerated the procedure well. The patient was taken to the Intensive Care Unit intubated with a stable blood pressure .

████████████████

DICTATING FOR:

████████████████

TR: jyy DD: 07/30/96 TD: 07/31/96 2:51 P
CC: ████████████████

EMERGENCY ASSOC TRAUMA
████████████████

Date of Surgery Corrected 08/02/96/dv

POLICE DEPARTMENT

OFFICER'S REPORT

PAGE 1 of 2 PAGES

CRIME OR INCIDENT	*Domestic A&B - Poss CLASS D - ARREST*
LOCATION	███████
APT.	
PRINCIPAL PARTY	███████
HOME PHONE	
BUS. PHONE	
ADDRESS	███████

ACTION TAKEN – CHECK BOX BELOW

ARREST #1	X	CHARLES A. PEABODY JR.	AGE 20	SS # ███████
		███████		DOB 03-21-77
ARREST #2				SS #
				DOB

WARRANT	M/V ACC. FORM	TRAFFIC DUTY	COURT	CIVIL	PARKING COMPLAINT
SUMMONS	FELONY FORM	M/V TOWED	TOW CO.	OWNER NOTIFIED	REG. #
M/V VIOL.		M/V TOWED	TOW CO.	OWNER NOTIFIED	REG. #

DETAILS OF CRIME OR INCIDENT

Dispatched by radio to above location on report of a family disturbance. On arrival with Officer ███ we were met by ███████ Age 52, outside entrance to driveway of residence. Mr. Peabody stated there was no problem and that a previous family matter had been resolved. Near the entrance of the residence I heard a male voice screaming, later observed to be def. Charles Peabody Jr. and a female voice, ███ Peabody age 44. The screaming by def appeared very hostile and threatening. Officer ███ and I approached front of residence and I observed Def ran inside house and lock the door. Def was asked numerous times to open the door but def refused. I requested Patrol Supervisor, Sgt ███ to meet Officers at residence.

Spoke to ███ Peabody age 23, who I found crying, in/on the front lawn. ███ stated her brother, def went crazy and smashed furniture and household items on the first floor of residence. ███ stated, def shoved and pushed her, and slapped Mother ███ numerous times in the face.

Def opened door, and Officer ███ and I went inside. I observed that the interior of house had furniture over turned and smashed. ███████ arrest for Dom A&B. During booking of above by myself one ███████

REPORTING OFFICER	███████	UNIT ███	SUPERVISOR ███████
2ND OFFICER	███		

POLICE DEPARTMENT

OFFICER'S REPORT

| REPORT # ████████ |
| DATE 03/28/97 |
| TIME 2005 |
| PAGE 2 of 2 PAGES |

CRIME OR INCIDENT

DETAILS OF CRIME OR INCIDENT

located in rear pant pocket by Officer ████ Def charged with Pos. class D, marijuana.

Spoke to parents with Sgt ████ at residence. Parents state Def has emotional and physical problems from a fatal MV accident that he survived. Parents state family has been in counseling for approx a year.

All parties advised of victim rights of 209A Abuse Law.

Ext damage to interior of residence in the thousands of dollars.

████████ stated no assault took place to her person by son, Charles Jr. She did state she was fearful of her son's "outburst".

6

AN ALLERGY AND A MENTAL

OBSESSION

I did nothing for the first three days up North but chain smoke

cigarettes. The staff refused to treat me until some of the fog burned

off. Finally, after ripping apart my perception of conventional recovery

and mainstream AA, I was offered a solution that really works. They

began reading the Big Book of Alcoholics Anonymous to me like I was

a child, or rather, a student. They taught me that I could recover

completely… and for good. I don't have to live forever "in recovery."

There is hope for me and for every addict in the world.

The beginning of the Big Book contains a letter from Dr.

William D. Silkworth, who repeatedly treated AA's co-founder, Bill

Wilson, at Charles B. Towns hospital in New York. Towns Hospital

was once a giant in the field of drug and alcohol addiction. But the

doctor admits to the public and concedes to himself that he cannot help

most chronic alcoholics and drug addicts despite a slew of medical and pharmaceutical options. He admits that advances in science and clinical treatment cannot effect change the way this spiritual program can. Inherent in his argument is the idea that "moral psychology" must be taken to cause sufficient change in the hopeless drunk. Man-made remedies often fail to change an addict into a better person. He is filthy from negative and destructive behaviors, thoughts and words. He is a caldron of mental illness and spiritual decay. He may have to grow from deep within to fully recover. He may have to live by moral principles. He may need something that isn't tangible.

So addiction isn't my fundamental problem. The problem is spiritual. To be less abstract, it's a life problem. Addicts refuse to live life on life's terms. They refuse to grow up and walk through pain that everybody feels. They feel entitled to remain in their comfort zones even if doing so comes at the expense of others. They refuse to do things that push them outside of themselves. And so if my illness is spiritual in nature, then so must be my solution.

Two fellow losers and I sat in an old, grungy room armed with a podium and chalkboard. The staffer looked at us. Time to smash a 1st Step into our brains.

"Okay, you've achieved physical sobriety. Now what? What are you going to do?"

We shrugged our shoulders.

"Now what?" he says? I have absolutely no idea.

"Okay, so you have two problems besides the underlying soul sickness. One is physical; the other is mental. Physically, you're screwed. Your body is damaged goods."

Great, that's nice.

"You have an *allergy* to drugs and alcohol."

Here's the allergy: I put a drug into my body and bang! Something happens. I snap when a drug, *any* drug, enters my bloodstream and saturates my brain. It takes hold of every atom of my being. I experience what the doctor who wrote to Alcoholics Anonymous refers to as the "phenomenon of craving" - a biological craving that supersedes any desire to stop. Nothing matters except more. The idea of having two shots of booze and stopping is absolute torture. Why even start unless there is enough to get obliterated and pass out? My wife has a sip of wine and puts the glass down. What the hell is that all about? I just don't get it. I hurl mine down, then hers, then yours, then the rest of the bottle in the fridge, then I break into Pa's house at two in the morning to steal his booze, and on and on until I'm out cold, in jail, or dead.

It's not your typical allergy where you break out into hives, fever, anaphylactic shock. Nope. I break out into ease and comfort. All of the sudden I feel normal. All of the sudden my mind slows down and I can handle life, go to work, listen to you tell me about your day. So I break out into more. Sober, I can't handle anything. You talk to me and all I hear is "blah, blah, blah…" If anything does pass through my mind, it's *when are you going to shut up so I can go get jammed?*

But the real crux of my problem was what the Big Book referred to as a *mental obsession.* One staffer defined it as "recurring thoughts or ideas that don't respond to ration or reason." You can simply define this as insanity. I'm going along, everything is okay, no problem whatsoever… then I'm in your bathroom and I see some painkillers and not even a thought passes through my head. I reach out, grab the bottle and throw 'em down. No conversations with my better half. No debating. Like a gun firing, it's all or none. In those moments, the mind goes blank and 'choice' is no longer an ability that I carry. In those moments, everything I know about my tragic history just disappears. In those moments, insane thoughts seem reasonable and normal.

Well, it's okay 'cause I'm just doing Percocet and not OxyContin.

Then: *Well I'm still okay because I'm only doing OxyContin and not heroin.*

Then: *I'm definitely okay because I'm not shooting heroin, I'm just sniffing it.*

Finally: *I know I'm okay because I'm not homeless, toothless, and rotting away in some crack house.*

Yes I know that I shouldn't blow heroin, yes I know it's wrong and I'll ruin everything, but I don't care. And even if I do care and I don't want to lose my wife, job, family, savings… I go do it anyway. Put a drug in front of me and I turn into a dumpster, consuming everything in sight. I can't stop. Nothing can stop me. You can't stop me. Mom can't stop me. Doctors can't stop me. Pills can't stop me. Wayne Dyer and Deepak Chopra can't stop me. Nothing human or man-made can stop me. I'm basically screwed.

Over the years, of course, counselors told me that I relapse because of triggers. Let's be clear: There is no such thing as a trigger. Nothing has to happen to make me want to use. I want to use all the time. In other words, everything is a trigger. Breathing is a trigger.

A trigger is just a flimsy excuse. It could be anything. It's 2:00 in the afternoon - I need to get high. Just took a shower - I need to get high. I'm happy - need to get high. I'm angry – need to get high. It's partly cloudy - good reason to get high. It's partly sunny - good reason. I woke up - definitely a good reason. Existing, you see, is the only trigger I need.

Counselors are one thing, but the PhDs always loved to dig in and find THE REASON.

"Charlie, there must be a reason why you use. What is it, son? Is it the depression? Your family? Abuse? Were you hurt in some way? Are you angry?"

Doctors, counselors, social workers, families, spouses, and non-addicts will go on trying to understand why we use the way we do, despite the consequences. Let me save everybody the trouble: There is no reason why addicts use and alcoholics drink. It's not because I'm angry, sad, anxious, depressed, shy, emotionally withdrawn, or feel so alone. It's not because I have ADHD, or bipolar disorder, or major depression, or some personality disorder. It's not because of my parents or my "crazy" family.

It's not because I was abused by babysitters who stuck me in an inch of cold water, or who called me a child of Satan for pissing outside, or who physically assaulted me, or who made me brush my teeth every time I ate a marshmallow, or who left me home alone, or who stole my money to abandon me and go out with their boyfriend. It's not because the cool kid pissed on my head when I wanted to hang out with his group of friends. It's not because I was jumped and attacked three times in Vermont during college. It's not because my Dad is an isolated and depressed alcoholic who didn't hang out with me much. It's not because he was prone to fits of rage and dragged my sister around the house. It's not because of my genes or any predisposition to alcoholism or depression. Even if that were scientifically true, which it now appears to be, I'd never have set it off in the first place had I not drunk over and over and over. Nothing in this world is responsible for me becoming a drug addict and an alcoholic beside myself. And I put a hell of a lot of time and effort into my achievement.

The best advice addiction specialists and modern AA has to offer is to tell addicts and alcoholics to avoid people, places and things that make them want to use. Fantastic. Now I have to stay away from everything and everyone *and* I'm completely miserable. What a life! If that were my fate, I'd have to spend all my time planning how to get from my house to work.

Hmm… I can't go down this street because my buddy lives there and I got high there once, but I also can't go down that street because one of my dealers lives there. Hmm... I can't go this way

because there's a liquor store on the corner, and hmm... I can't go that

way because I had a really good time using at that park one day. Gee, I

guess I can't go anywhere. I guess the only way I'll be able stay sober

is if I lock myself up in a cage and never go anywhere!

But guess what? That's not the kind of solution I'm looking for. How about being a free man no matter where I go?

This is precisely the reason that I wrote this book. For fifteen years, I have tried everything I could think of to get better and have failed. Why? Why do roughly 1 in 30 addicts actually stay sober after conventional forms of treatment? That is one horrible statistic.

The first problem is listening to other people. Especially anyone who is not a recovered addict. Take therapy for example, a treatment method that allows me to continue doing absolutely nothing. Sure I gain insights about myself, but do I walk out of the door and apply what I've learned? Dad blew tens of thousands of sweat-earned dollars sending me to top of the line psychologists and psychiatrists. Poor guy. It may sound silly, but the reason it failed is because all we did was talk. Sorry, talking is not a solution. Addicts talk enough, in and out of therapy. I realize that talking *is* the therapeutic method, but it's virtually useless for someone whose primary concern in life is obtaining drugs and getting high. I left my 55-minute sessions totally unequipped and with no instructions other than to show up the following week. How am I supposed to apply psychology without the tools or the power to do so?

Next up, we have the self-help book method. I was a walking self-help book, with shelves that ranged from Buddhist meditation to healing the child within, from Christian mysticism to Ayurvedic remedies for depression, from creative visualization for my psychic scars to embracing the dark night of the soul. But will the books alone change me, or fix me, or make God present in my life?

How many times did I sit in bed at night reading an old sage's insights about not judging the thoughts in my mind and think, *Yes, that's it! I just discovered the sword by which to conquer all my depression and addiction forever*, only to wake up the next morning completely miserable and stuck in the same muddy pit of self-pity, frustration, and emptiness. Were all the books wrong? Of course not. It's more like I didn't so much as move an inch when it came to applying this stuff. Plus I'm not a Buddhist, or a born-again Christian, or a whatever. I'm a drug addict. I need a solution for drug addiction.

What about Methadone maintenance? Doesn't that at least keep me off the streets? What a tragedy. Still chained to addiction, there is no difference between Charlie on heroin and Charlie on Methadone. I'm jammed either way, so what happens really?

How about some elaborate combination of psychotropic medications? Okay, how about I just put up a brick wall between me and getting better, a wall between me and God? There is no spiritual experience on drugs. Given the effects to my biochemistry, ingesting psychotropic drugs made it increasingly more difficult to heal or to be honest. What good is it to be blocked, numbed, and less than clear? Medications fueled my reluctance to do the hard work, let alone do it with purity, clarity, or thoroughness. Nope, meds weren't powerful enough to expel this obsession. Besides, unless I take them forever, once I stop, I'm right back where I started - insane and untreated.

I also tried exercise routines. I got sober, went for a run, felt the endorphin rush, and thought I found the solution. *I'll just go to the gym everyday!* Okay fine, but what happens if I can't go one day? And, oh yeah, I forgot that I'm still destitute inside. Soon I sink back into depression. Then I relapse again.

I tried eating organic food, eating vegetarian, eating vegan. I tried St. John's wart and a homeopathy called Lycopodium for the hole in my aura. I tried Outward Bound and being outside doing things I love such as hiking and rock-climbing. I tried playing and composing music, writing poems and stories. I tried acting in theatre. I tried socializing more. I tried socializing less. I moved to Vermont. I moved back. I drove across the country. I drove back. I moved into Boston and got a job. I tried girlfriends. Maybe falling in love will get me better? But I relapse no matter what I try. Every imaginable remedy I have tried and failed.

There is a fundamental problem with conventional treatment strategies: The thinking is backwards. Cognitive behavioral therapy (CBT) professes to identify the faulty belief, change the belief, and act accordingly. Can we really expect an addict to change his faulty beliefs as he is? Do mental exercises really have the power to change the thinking of an addicted lunatic?

Sometimes he must act his way into right thinking rather than try to think his way into right action. Crazy can't think straight, but there's fuel in action, and eventually the mind follows.

That idea isn't my own, as is the case with so many others. My sponsor is the one who worded it so beautifully, so for the record, he said to a group of people one night, "If I can't think my way into right action… then I must act my way into right thinking."

7

ADDICT CRYSTALLIZED

The first time I ate an OxyContin, a switch went off in my head. I knew right then: I was BORN to do this. As the opiate saturated my central nervous system, a great calm washed over me. Every molecule of my physical and mental being enjoyed freedom from even the slightest discomfort. I was simultaneously released from all anxiety, depression, pain and anguish. OxyContin is basically synthetic heroin, although it's legally prescribed as a painkiller. The effect is the best of both worlds: the physical comfort of booze without the falling down, loss of control, sick feeling, and the mental comfort of weed without the self-consciousness or paranoia. With OxyContin in my blood, I could do anything. I could speak to other people with greater confidence. I could work all day. I could run around and play sports. I could last longer with women. I was THE MAN. Everything was perfect.

I was twenty-one years old and newly enrolled at the University of Massachusetts Boston following my UVM disaster and a summer of minimal sobriety. Dressing up in Brooks Brothers suits, pretending to be a corporate hustler who never finished his bachelor's degree was my new thing. Overexcited, gregarious, and reaching the borders of mania from all the heavy drinking, people found me understandably annoying. A girl on campus came right out with it. After ten years, I can still remember her exact words.

"I don't like you."

"Me? Why?"

"I don't know what it is. I just don't like you."

"Huh… well, coming from you that's like a compliment."

Even some of my college professors took issue with my demeanor, like the Spanish professor who went around the room asking us why we were taking her class. I thought it might be amusing to give her an honest response.

"Me gustan las mujeres espanolas y quiero aprender el idioma para poder obtener las ninas espanol."

Translation: I love Spanish girls and want to learn the language so I can pick them up.

If I was ever honest as a drug addict, it was only at the exact wrong time. She took offense, threatened a sexual harassment charge, and barely passed me with a D- despite near perfect grades.

It was a gorgeous fall afternoon when the phone call came in from an old buddy. Paying little attention to my conscience, I blew off a set of afternoon classes that Dad so generously financed and sped out of Boston to pick up my friend for a round of golf. As he stepped into my car, he pulled out a small, orange colored pill. It read OC on one side and 20 on the other. The orange color coating is a time-release mechanism, which can be easily moistened and rubbed off, or simply bit into, thereby releasing all 20 milligrams of active drug chemical into the body.

"Here, take this. You'll love it. Don't even chew it; just swallow it whole. I shouldn't give this to you 'cause you'll love it so much you won't stop. But you have to try this."

"Sign me up."

I ate it. A fleeting feeling that it was wrong to eat the pill tried to penetrate my better half, but at that point in my life it was all too easy to shrug off that sort of thing.

Somewhere during the front nine, the OC 20 kicked in and I was showered by a rush of pure bliss. I was top to bottom saturated with euphoria. In that moment, I gave my heart and soul to OxyContin. I loved it and protected it like a family member. I found all that I needed in life. I could now handle those things that I could never handle before - everything.

For the rest of the fall, I left school early everyday to eat OCs and play golf. Arming myself with a golf cart, a twelve pack, a bag of weed, and opiates flowing through my brain and central nervous system was my favorite thing to do on earth. Nothing was better.

In two months, I was a chronic user, eating or sniffing three, five, seven a day - every fucking one I could get my hands on, but elementary stuff compared to what my addiction morphed into over the next several years.

I knew it was wrong and expensive but I didn't give a shit. Even after shedding my first forty pounds, I knew that I could fix everything once I got jammed again, you know what I mean? No, perhaps you don't. I forget that you might be normal. The rationale is: More OxyContin in my blood = the ability to calmly and sanely approach my problem.

So over the course of a lovely New England autumn, gradually the semester at UMASS Boston, the 4.00 GPA, the honors psychology standing, the nomination for the Morris K. Udall Scholarship for Excellence in Environmental Studies, the once lesion-less skin, and all other accomplishments took a back seat for good. I was still excelling in my head.

Another presenting problem: when you use opiates or heroin all day, every day, you sort of appear as though you're suffering from a delusional, psychosomatic disorder where bugs are eating you alive. All I did was itch myself. It was embarrassing. Bloody scratches, scabs, and scars covered my body, especially around the hip area. Jammed out of my mind, I spent hours at night gouging away. It's disgusting.

That winter of 1998-99, I cleaned myself up. Three weeks of physical sobriety was enough to drown me in another crippling bout of depression. It also pounded my soul in the winter for the first time, thus erasing my presumed insight about how the summer heat was directly responsible for my depression.

To dispel my self-inflicted misery, I tried having a go at the geographical cure. I took settlement money from the car accident of 1996 and rented a studio in Boston's Back Bay neighborhood. Believe it or not, my realtor was actually a decent guy, considering the endless and seedy pool of real estate agents he's up against. He told me I should work for him during the busy summer season. A job? What a lovely idea to enlighten and mature the man-child who is Charles Peabody. So I went at once to enroll in a weekend crash course, sailed through a multiple-choice exam, and obtained my real estate license.

That license helped me progress into a hopeless drug addict. I could make the kind of money I needed to keep the runs I went on longer. It also allowed my tolerance to grow to absurd lengths. The fact that it made me worse was a blessing, in a sense, because the worse I got, the closer I came to getting better. I may never have the life I have now had I not rotted away, year after year, in the dirty depths of opiate addiction, alcoholism, and apartment rentals. Perhaps God smiled as I grew worse, knowing that with every line of heroin, I drew closer to Him.

The real estate industry twisted my personality and distorted my overall frame of reference. For me, it was a self-serving and spiritless job. I became the guy I loved hating - a zombie, or fellow member of the bottom rung scum of the world of sales and money. I dressed up in fancy clothes that I couldn't afford. I fed people a soliloquy of bullshit everyday so I could pickpocket their hard-earned money just for opening up a door. I was quick and cocky.

116

I showed up to my new gig, rented a shitload of apartments, and made all kinds of money. I was proud and self-sustainable. The job knocked me out of depression by inserting more false confidence. But confidence is not always the best thing for a drug addict. Charlie doing well is the equivalent of Charlie standing on the edge of a cliff with a little voice behind me whispering, "Go ahead, jump! Sabotage, Sabotage! SABOTAGE!"

You see, with all the cash coming in, I felt like I had the right to do exactly as I pleased. Therefore, only a brief interval of time stood between the end of my workday and twelve cold beers in my gut. I drank like a fish. I drank alone in my apartment. I liked it that way. No one could tell me how inappropriate I was. No one could tell me that I had a problem. I didn't have to expose myself to concerned friends. And I could sweat out the alcohol during the day while running around showing crap apartments in Back Bay.

I set up my new apartment like a jungle. Enormous palm trees overhung the mantle, hanging plants dropped down from the ceiling, old furniture I took from Dad's house lined a large Persian rug. It looked like a rich man's opium den. I loved it. I blasted music all day and night as I slowly spiraled into a manic haze of alcohol-induced psychosis. The poor woman upstairs couldn't stand my music, especially at volumes that cause ear damage. She banged on the floor incessantly... so I turned it up. I loved my place. I was happy. The only shitty days were the ones I spent hour upon hour on all fours inspecting my rug for specs of cocaine or weed.

My tolerance to alcohol was most exceptional. I awoke every morning to complete a daily cycle of conditioned responses designed to ward off depression, the first of which was immediately cracking open a Sam Adams. To face the bathroom mirror, it was necessary to put down the better half of a six-pack and rip a few bong hits. Only then was I was ready to shower, get dressed, and keep up the charade as a corporate player.

On went the Brooks Brother's suit, custom Italian loafers, and plenty of Crew gel to get the Euro-Hollywood-wet-hair-look that I delicately primed for the disinterested community of Boston. I wanted people to think I was successful and famous. Being a fake is one of the great thrills of drinking.

Then I skipped off to lunch at one of the image-obsessed watering holes on Newbury Street, which consisted of a couple martinis. Sometimes I ate. Sometimes I just stared at the menu.

Afternoons called for mild thirst quenchers. A half a bottle of pinot grigio was usually sufficient to crawl through the next couple hours.

The sun fell and I thanked God for a normal time to drink. I got spoiled with all my real estate commissions and had a liter of Belvedere vodka and a case of Sam Adams delivered every night from a package store on Newbury Street. I had about $15,000 saved up from real estate deals, so I could drink what I wanted.

A few cocktails at home base and it was time to enter the public arena again to see how far I could go before getting 86'd from bars or restaurants. Two packs of Marlboros didn't help much either, especially with the asthma. But smoking cigarettes was the perfect adult pacifier when sucking my thumb was no longer developmentally appropriate.

My girlfriend at the time went to law school. She was only moderately depressed and on reduced medication, so all in all she was pretty normal. She lived with her sister in an apartment that my company rented to them. They appeared every month to drop off a rent check, and as soon as I bumped into the cute one at a bar one night, that was that.

The not-so-cute one craved getting me out of her sister's life like you'd want a ghost out of the house. To her, I was 'Charlie the monster'. Over macaroni one night, the cute one suddenly went on one of her own vocal adventures, asserting that her father had hired a private investigator to perform a background check and follow me around Boston. Delusional and melodramatic, I believed her and indulged my imagination to utmost. Given that I considered myself to be extremely important, I actually enjoyed this sort of thing.

It all culminated one night as I rode my fantasy of being followed. I noticed an open window in an abandoned apartment across the street, which confirmed my theory that it was surely the lookout for a private investigator. I called 911 to report my lunatic story. Within minutes, I went from watching the Red Sox on my couch to completely spun out of my mind.

The Boston police phoned Mom, who rushed over to my apartment with her new boyfriend. As I spotted the beacon of sanity and clarity, shame began spewing out through my pores. The presence of her alone patronized and embarrassed me. So I figured the best way out of this one was to try convincing the cops that it was none other than Mom who was trespassing, spying on me, and God knows what else. Sweet little Mom became the target of my drunken, manic tirade.

I guess I should mention that I later shut my mother out of my life for a good year or so because she was concerned about my mental state after declaring that I was going to buy a $10,000 engagement ring for my future wife with no money to actually pay for it. That's right, I cut Mom off altogether… no phone calls, no letters, not even a thought or prayer. This is the same Mom who gave me the world, the same Mom who nourished me with loving-kindness, the same Mom who brought me bananas and milk in the middle of the night when I suffered from growing pains.

The Boston police soon realized that Mr. Charlie Peabody was the only one present with some immediate issues. And fortunately for the general public, off to the emergency room I went, tied down inside an ambulance once a local Judge signed the pink slip. Massachusetts Law, chapter 123, section 12 exists for the "emergency restraint of dangerous persons; application for hospitalization examination." Massachusetts Law, chapter 123, section 35 exists for "involuntary commitment of alcoholics or substance abusers."

Two days later, I woke up chained to a floor in four-point restraints at a psychiatric hospital in one of those white padded rooms you think only exist in the movies. Trying to shake off the fog, I realized my hands and feet were locked to a floor. I lost my fucking mind.

"Get your filthy hands off of me you dumb fuck!"

"He's still out of control. Better shoot him up again. You don't want to calm down, Mr. Peabody? That's fine. Maybe another day or two."

"Stupid monkey! Who the fuck raised you anyway?"

Thorazine. Haldol. Phenobarbital. Choose one. Out cold for another day and a half.

I woke up to a combination of mood stabilizers, antipsychotics, anxiolytics, and a charmed misdiagnosis of bipolar disorder. Sure I *looked* bipolar. High almighty with a decent supply, I am exuberant. All out, I'm absolutely miserable. Addicts often mimic bipolar behavior and are frequently misdiagnosed.

Besides, why give me (a drug addict) a diagnosis? Now I have a clinical excuse to justify my selfish and destructive behavior.

"Sorry I totaled your car Dad, but it's not my fault because I have bipolar disorder. It's the bipolar's fault."

"Bipolar drove to Dorchester, bought a gram of heroin, and sniffed the whole thing, honey, not me!"

"Sorry I just called you a controlling, crazy bitch, Mom, but it's not really me. It's the disorder I have."

Ah... okay, sure.

My poor roommate at the asylum was regularly treated with electroconvulsive shock therapy. The look in his eyes when he returned was unmistakable, appearing as though someone had just raped and tortured him. Following the shock treatments, he remained suicidal for days. Sometimes he just ran away. Staffers usually found him running down the street in his pajamas.

The other guests were usually talking to the walls or indulging violent schizophrenic outbursts. I was an alcoholic. But not in the eyes of the nationally recognized psychiatrist who diagnosed me.

How do I know of the tragic mistreatment of addicts? Because they fed me Ativan three times a day, along with Depakote and Zyprexa. Depakote is a mood-stabilizer, and other than reorganizing your brain chemistry, it's only moderately damaging. Zyprexa is an anti-psychotic but also has a moderate sedative effect. Ativan is a benzodiazepine. Benzodiazepines like Valium, Xanax and Klonopin are modern day replacements for barbiturates (tranquilizers) because they do not depress respiratory functioning. They do, however, get you as high as you can possibly imagine. Whoopee! I crushed them up, sniffed them, mixed them with other drugs, got jammed out of my mind, and wound up with a nice little habit all over again. Good job, Doc.

Free tip to doctors: Don't treat drug addicts with mood altering substances. Just a suggestion.

That fall was the fall of 9/11. While most of the country was mourning or giving service in the aftermath of a great tragedy, I gave myself permission to slip into another severe depression. I think it's worthwhile noting that this depression was by far my worst, and ironically followed a lethargic summer as a post-nuthouse zombie on all of their show-stopping medications.

And when I say worst, I mean really bad. I sunk to new levels of paralysis as my depression morphed into something entirely new. No spark of life or spirit as there used to be during the intense, racy moments of my early depressions. Nope. None of that. Inside lay a cold, silent void. An ocean separated me from God. I stopped caring altogether.

On good days, I pulled myself out of bed by two or three o'clock in the afternoon, though typically it was getting dark before I stood up. When night fell, it became more depressing to stay in the sack, so I conjured enough willpower to peel myself off my mattress and have some eggs.

I withdrew from every class for the fall semester at UMASS Boston. The one thing I managed to do on occasion was go see a therapist at 4:30 p.m. on Tuesday afternoon, which meant I had to get up early, around 3:45 p.m. That's it.

Other than those brutal Tuesdays, I sat withdrawn and isolated in my apartment trying to escape myself by watching sappy movies and chain-smoking Camel Lights. I delighted only in finding a new position in bed during the afternoon hours that allowed me to drift back to sleep for a while. I awoke frequently to an immediate feeling of dread. And so I lived only for the momentary escape of being out cold. Sure there was no conscious experience of sleep, but it was just such a tremendous pleasure NOT to be awake.

For the couple hours of daylight I was awake for (good days), I sat in my chair staring out of the window watching normal people and trying to comprehend them. I couldn't fathom how they had the energy to get up, make phone calls, meet up with friends, go out, walk around, work, talk, interact, play, laugh, live.

How are they all so okay? Are they really that happy? No, they must all be pretending. Doesn't everyone feel totally leveled by depression? I mean why bother doing anything at all?

Even around my closest friends, shame spewed out through my pores. Trying to interact was sheer torture. I was only safe in reclusion.

Bottom line: I was too embarrassed to leave my apartment. I hated doing anything unless I felt strong enough or was at least able to fake it. Being a fake was okay, but being vulnerable in public was out of the fucking question. I figured it was safer to just stay inside and even though nothing happens, I might somehow randomly die. Then it hit me that I wouldn't just die, at least not without a ton of balls - balls I didn't have. So I retreated back into a paralysis of fear. That's how it was, day after day after day… until my soon-to-be wife called me up out of the blue.

Future Wife had an unstoppable will to travel, though she made a pit stop back home in Massachusetts to pick up some garbage. The combination of our blooming friendship and a new real estate gig pulled me out of my horrendous city funk. I left the concrete jungle every weekend to relax and nourish my soul on the beautiful coastline of the north shore. I even found a plentiful stash of painkillers in my future mother in-law's bathroom drawer. All in all, it was a tremendous summer. No more depression, money was rolling in, days on the beach were long, good friends were abundant, and more importantly, golf and

OxyContin showered me with relief. But rapid progression stops for no one. Neither do the mistakes.

I left my old Saab in neutral and ran into future mother-in-law's house to hunt for a missing OC 80, only to come back out to see Dad's fifth vehicular investment rolling down the long driveway and smashing into a not so welcoming tree. Good opportunity to purchase a newer Saab, which gave me that infantile feeling of arrival. Dad co-signed for the loan. Totaled in three weeks flat. And no comprehensive insurance after neglecting to fill out a vehicle inspection report. Five years at $300 a month sounds like a curse, but for a man-child like me, I suppose it was kind of a bitter blessing.

My thinking was typically off that night, having just purchased 20 Klonopin from a local citizen of none other than Peabody, Massachusetts. I came up with this cool idea that if I quickly eat about half of the pills and jump into my car, they won't kick in until I get back to my new residence at Future Wife's aunt's house. The idea may not have been so bad if I had just left out the six-pack and the OC 40s, but hey, I never said I was a psychopharmacologist.

The plan failed when I passed out while driving through the stuffy town of Hamilton and uprooted a traffic light pole. Hitting the vertical bar of steel woke me up and I was thrilled to see that my car had slid off the pole and was still running well enough to get away. The mangled Saab flickered on and off, jerking forward all the way to the aunt's house. More unfortunate was the responding officer who followed an oil trail and had the job of confronting one of my classic stupors. Future Wife's aunt found me in the kitchen, head flat down on the table, clinging to a bottle of her bourbon.

Adding to my criminal record, I managed to tack on a few more (dismissed) charges for destruction of public property and leaving the scene of an accident. Needless to say, the aunt, the responding officer, and the entire police station made the top of my 8th Step amends list years later.

After a good introduction of how marriage would look, next I was able to ruin what was supposed to be one of the most special nights of Future Wife's life. She opened her first event in New York City to show her abstract paintings. It was a small and intimate affair attended by no more than family and close friends. My plan was to surprise her by taking a train to Manhattan and pulling off the proposal of a lifetime.

I stepped onto the train at South Station looking like I'd been run over. My skin was covered with lesions - gouges I made from scratching my face. Gaunt and sickly wouldn't even begin to describe my appearance. I thought I had enough OxyContin to last the whole week, but whoops! Just sniffed the last one off the train seat. I sat there, nodding off, daydreaming about somehow finding more.

Reduced to a few cigarettes, a hit of weed, and some change, my excitement sprouted again when spotting a bar on the train. Minor consolation, however, as it failed to ward off the oncoming opiate withdrawals. Still high, though a bit under-slept, I grew sick and started sweating profusely.

When I arrived in New York, it was pouring outside. I walked a mile or two in the wind and rain and arrived at the art show appearing like death itself. I saw myself in the reflection of the café window and hardly recognized the image projected back at me. I was skeletal... my eyes sunken into my head, skin pale and discolored. I almost considered not going in, but that wasn't my style. Not even the few normal brain cells I had left were going to tell *me* what to do.

Everyone was dressed up. It was quiet. I walked in and heads turned. Future Wife stood shocked and stunned. Infuriated and ashamed, she covered it up and pretended everything was fine. That's the moment she began the act that her dope sick wreck of a future husband was perfectly normal. But making an ass of myself didn't stop me from my big surprise. There I was with a cheap ring, sinking further into opiate withdrawal and sopping wet. What girl could refuse such pure romance? I found it shocking when she had some issues to take up before any sort of proposal would be considered. I mean come-on, I came all this way for the surprise of a lifetime!

Future Wife knew me long before I mutated into an emaciated, chronically addicted asshole. She wanted so much to just take care of me and make wholesome dinners to heal my shriveled body. Warm, organic meals were prepared every night. Feeding me in bed one night, she went to clean up the kitchen only to return a moment later to find me passed out with food mashed into the covers and streaming down my face. I wonder if that was more disturbing than waking up to a soaking bed later on - too intoxicated, lazy, or sick to notice myself peeing all over the mattress and the leg of my fiancé.

The one formal request Future Wife made was being with her when we saw her family, and perhaps even presenting myself like a stable, productive person. Instead, I walked into family dinners like I ruled the world. Dynamics changed in an instant. People were uncomfortable. I made inappropriate comments and gestures. I challenged people intellectually. I'm not sure what I was trying to prove, always acting a hundred times more successful than I was. Wearing a suit that falls off you as you walk to the bathroom is not the best way to impress in-laws. But they suffered through it, most of them oblivious. I don't think Future Wife was too oblivious. She was absolutely petrified of the next words out of my mouth. Family dinners were intense, panicked, humiliating.

"Yup, just made like ten grand in a day. How you doing? Do you guys have any clue what kind of fucking IQ you're dealing with? Wait a minute, you realize what family I come from, don't you? No? Well, that's okay. I certainly can't expect to be constantly be surrounded by people who are up to par… ahahahahaha. No, no, kidding, kidding."

"Charlie, we've heard some disturbing things about your past. Is it true you were abusive to your x-girlfriend?"

"Excuse me? I'd like to know how you are able to make such assertions when you have the brain of an empty trashcan?

"Charlie, don't you have a history of chemical imbalance?"

"The only thing imbalanced is the way you selfishly plow through your life at the expense of your neglected, terrified daughters."

Horrified by the prospect of marrying a sleeping monster, Future Wife's relatives were forced to engage in low-road tactics. False rumors went out about barroom indiscretions, stories were concocted about x-girlfriend physical abuse, background checks and private investigations surfaced as appropriate methods. Accusations of a flawed mental health history were, fortunately, the only accurate judgments. I'm happy to report that my in-laws have since become friends who trust and respect me, but this is the bone-crushing ripple effect that the addict's behavior has on those who are trapped inside his lunatic world.

Engaged with less than a year before the wedding, I had to start bringing in some money. I've always had a tendency to resort to menial labor when vulnerable, depressed, or financially insecure, so I worked for a local moving company, and wouldn't you know it, my whole crew turned out to be drug addicts. I showed up on day one and hopped into the truck. The foreman looked at me, and this is exactly what he said.

"By the way, if you like painkillers then stay away from me, pal, 'cause I got a little problem right now."

"Excuse me? That's like music to my ears. Sign me up, bro."

"Seriously. I don't want to mess you up. I know you gotta girl and everything."

"Mess me up? Hahaha… That's a good one."

Painkillers went to OxyContin and OxyContin went to heroin. I remember looking at that line of heroin thinking I cannot and will not ever put this evil into my body. About two minutes later, it was gone. The next day, I was buying tangy, brown dope from an x-con who liked smoking fish half naked outside his mother's house. Every morning, we made a convenient detour so we could sniff a half gram of heroin before moving people's crap around. And the $10,000 winning scratch ticket didn't help much either.

In an effort to stop sniffing dope, I bought Methadone and was addicted immediately. Methadone, commonly and falsely thought of as an opiate blocker, is actually chemically considered to be a synthetic opioid, thus acting on the same receptors as morphine-based opiates like heroin or OxyContin. Methadone "maintenance" as a form of treatment is used in many state and federally funded programs to treat heroin addicts. It is highly addictive, causing serious and extended side effects including nausea, vomiting, diarrhea, fever, chills, tremors, severe joint pain, tachycardia, and psychological agony/cognitive effects including suicidal ideation, severe depression, paranoia, delusion and panic disorder, just to name a few. I loved it. I ate 160 to 200 milligrams (a lot) everyday and turned back into a rail. No one likes to be around that kind of weight loss.

The wedding was a month away, but my golden rule in life was not to let anyone see me weak, insecure, or vulnerable. Ever. So I detoxed myself off the Methadone at home in bed. Some sound advice to any addicts out there: Don't ever do Methadone. Worst thing I've ever felt.

Having invested so much already, Future Wife had little choice but to get behind me. We bought ten, 40-milligram Methadone wafers and a bunch of Xanax from a friend who came to the rescue. We broke up the Methadone chips to wean me down by five milligrams a day. Xanax was for easing the withdrawals and getting some limited sleep.

As the Methadone begins to run out, all there is for relief is the Xanax... then all those are gone. First, all of my energy is sucked out of me. I'm beyond lethargic. My muscles feel like they weigh a thousand pounds. Moving anywhere becomes a struggle. Indescribable stomach pain begins, accompanied by sweats and chills. It's the middle of the summer, temperature in the mid-nineties, and I'm freezing. I go around in pants and four shirts on, including a flannel jacket. My clothes hang off me, and if it isn't clear that I'm a pathetic drug addict, I can easily be mistaken for a male anorexic.

The pain gets worse and worse and is loyally followed by psychological torture. I feel like I'm going crazy. I become so frustrated, I pull my hair out, punch myself in the head, and bang my

head against the wall. I hate myself.

No appetite either. I mean zero fucking appetite. The thought of

food makes me sicker and more depressed, forget about the constant

reminder that I've been reduced to a Methadone-sick waif, writhing in

bed. I try drinking a protein shake one morning. As soon as I gulp the

shake, I throw it back up into the glass. I try to swallow it again and

throw it up again. I manage to keep some down each time, so I repeat

this swallowing and puking process over and over until the chocolate-

flavored protein shake is gone. Protein shakes have to do it for a few

days because I just can't swallow food.

For some reason, I attempted a summer course at UMASS

Boston. I think I did it to feign productivity. Sweating and shaking, I

tried to participate, but while answering a question, I blacked out in

mid-sentence from a benzodiazepine seizure. Waking back up, I

apologized out loud to the entire room. Absolutely no idea how much

time had passed. I think all the normal people around me were so

boggled by my condition that they just sat there in dead silence. No one

looked in my direction. Not even the professor responded to my

awkward apology. The side effects of Methadone alone will cause an

addict to relapse or eat more, just to get out of the hell.

But I prayed selfishly and forced my way through it. I ran everyday, got a tan, worked out at the gym, drank protein shakes to gain weight, and smoked piles of weed. I was euphoric from kicking such God-awful evil. I was in ship shape for my wedding and sitting on a pink cloud of mania.

At the ceremony, I made sweeping promises to my almost wife. All the grandiose plans that went through my head, plans I so pompously showed off to everyone at the wedding, were backed by nothing. I acted like a hero who was off to conquer the world.

It worked. Everyone believed me. I fooled them all again. A dangerously good actor was now creeping through my blood. I had carefully crafted and built a great lie, and it worked for fifteen years. No one really knew. Not even Wife.

Despite my bullshit, our wedding day was a blessed occasion and took place on the most beautiful afternoon of the summer of 2003. We were married outside along the shore of Singing beach in Manchester, Massachusetts. Little compares to the beauty here. I proposed to her on the rocks about three times and, finally, there we were on the lawn of the quaint Singing Beach Club.

It was late August and the air had dried up after the mid-summer haze. She glided across the isle of grass like a glowing angel.

As she stepped up onto the altar, the sun broke through the clouds and shone down upon her face. Birds flew over us. I played my guitar and sang a song that I wrote to her. It was magical. We knew that despite my twisted addiction, all of this was slated. Our bond was undoubtedly blueprinted. It was the loveliest day of our years entrenched in my addiction.

Our honeymoon consisted of a) driving around in a rental car screaming at New York City cab drivers, b) trying to avoid damage to the rental car, and c) searching for Manhattan apartments the size of our closet back home in Gloucester, Massachusetts. Frustrated and flirting with depression, both of us were losing it. Like throwing darts on a map, I drove out of the city in any direction I saw fit and we ended up in a cozy little town that sits along the west side of the Hudson River. Just over the Tappan Zee Bridge, we pulled into the village of Nyack, New York and hastily rented an apartment.

Considering the shoeboxes we saw in Manhattan, I thought the new place was fantastic. Nevertheless, the floors had a film no industrial cleaning service could get off. The stink emanating from the kitchen was no other fault than the dead mice and dirty tampons stuck to an old glue trap under our oven. Dust built up at a pace unheard of.

And so we lived in a grungy attic for the next seven months, pretending to be okay.

I knew it in my heart: I was hollow. It didn't take a clinical psychologist to deduce that I was filled with false confidence and a warped self-image. My fragile self was quickly exposed as nothing more than the delusional fantasy I had to climb to the top of the acting world. It was a fantasy that crumbled before my first audition.

All I did with my days in New York was smoke pot, look for more pot, and go work out at the gym to pretend I was a supermodel. I still believed I was the most beautiful man in the world, so I gathered some energy and plowed my way into the top modeling agencies in New York, only to have my cocky bullshit shoved back in my face. It didn't take more than six months of this charade and a funneling of our savings to begin making plans to move back home to Massachusetts.

Resettled back in the north shore, I sank into another depression. Familiar territory at this point, I could now function through my depressions and complacently adjusted myself to the new norm. I did have to stop smoking pot for a while in order to get some kind of life going again. Unemployed and newly married with a desire for nothing else but weed is a fairly sad state of affairs.

I began to see myself as a flimsy shell of a man. I couldn't escape the reality that I'd just promised this girl everything in the world yet was doing absolutely nothing to strengthen my life, career, bank account, or perhaps the volcano of unresolved pain and mental illness.

I was determined to get another real estate gig and prove to my wife that I could act like a man. So on went the suit and tie. I then sauntered into a dirty office in the grungy Allston neighborhood of Boston and dished out all of my priceless experience, charisma, and professionalism. I didn't mention the complaint filed against me with the Better Business Bureau following one of my unethical rental deals in Back Bay in which I encouraged a client to forge his wife's signature on a lease in order to push it through. I was hired in minutes and scared shitless.

The place was disgusting. Used furniture, grossly stained rugs, peeling walls, and missing ceiling panels greeted any unfortunate client who passed through. The owner had one thing on his mind: money. Didn't matter how we made it. Besides, anyone willing to trust a guy who worked out of a shithole for an office had to be thoroughly lied to.

Fudging credit reports and other illegal methods became standard procedure. We cut out delinquent accounts, took Wite Out to credit scores, took information from good reports and recopied them onto bad ones, and then sent them off to landlords who really didn't give a shit anyway. I made $3,000 my first day and off I went.

I was sober for the longest time in years - about two months. Then the new guy showed up. He walked in and the first thing he said to me was absolutely priceless. "Hey man, nice to meet you. Oh hey, listen... I'm a heroin addict. I mean, I'm okay right now; well, actually I'm binging a little with a bottle of OC 10s I stole from my girlfriend's grandmother's house, but I'm fine. I just wanted to be honest with you in case you feel uncomfortable with that."

It was a beautiful summer afternoon. I had just made another few grand in commissions and nothing was wrong except for the usual empty feeling. As soon as the sound "OC 10" came out of his mouth, something happened. A single thought took me over in a split second. I couldn't think of anything else. Well before I made him give me one, I'd already relapsed.

The lesson? A sober man is just one very sick man. Achieving physical sobriety doesn't get us better at all. We can be sober for ten years and not change one bit. Nor are we immune from relapsing at any point in time and for no apparent reason. Sitting on my ass was a dangerous game to play. A broken mind and shattered spirit need to be fixed, and I'm now convinced that no human power can do that.

HOSPITAL

EMERGENCY SERVICES

AUTHORIZATION FOR TRANSFER

Directions: This form must be completed by a physician who authorizes transfer to another medical facility of a patient determined by the Emergency Department to have an emergency medical condition or to be in active labor. An emergency medical condition and active labor as defined by the Consolidated Omnibus Budget Reconciliation Act (COBRA) of 1985 (42USC1395dd) and amended by the Omnibus Budget Reconciliation Act.

PEABODY, CHARLES
DOB 3/21/77

3/30/01

SECTION 1	Complete as indicated.

A. ☑ The patient has been stabilized such that, within reasonable medical probability, no material deterioration of the patient's condition is like result from or occur during the transfer. (A patient in active labor has been stabilized if she has deliv including the placenta.)

B. ☐ Patient's condition has NOT been stabilized.

SECTION 2	Complete as indicated.

A. ☐ Reason for transfer: NOTE: If 1 (B) was checked, RISKS AND BENEFITS MUST ALSO BE LISTED BELOW

REMINDER: If the reason for transfer is because the on-call physician failed or refused to appear within a reason period of time, indicate the name and address of the on-call physician on the medical record.

psychiatric

SECTION 3	Complete only if Section 1 (B) above has been checked. If not, proceed to Section 4.

CHECK ONE OF THE FOLLOWING:

A. ☐ Patient requests transfer (or a legally responsible individual acting on the patient's behalf requests the transfer)
TRANSFER REQUEST BY UNSTABILIZED PATIENT on signature page of this form must be completed.

B. ☐ Medical benefits outweigh risks: Based on the reasonable risks and benefits to the patient, and based upon the information available at time of the patient's transfer, the medical benefits reasonably expected from the provision of appropri medical treatment at another medical facility outweigh the increased risks, if any, to the patient medi condition (including in the case of a pregnant woman, the risks to the unborn child(ren) from effecting transfer.

SECTION 4	Omit this section if 3 (A) was checked. Otherwise, complete A or B as appropriate.

A. ☐ Patient consents to the transfer (or a legally responsible individual acting on the patient's behalf consents to the transfer)
TRANSFER CONSENT on signature page of this form must be completed.

B. ☐ Transfer was offered but refused by the patient or a legally responsible individual acting on the patient's behalf
TRANSFER REFUSAL on a signature page of this form must be completed.

SECTION 5	Complete as indicated.

NOTE: The patient may not be transferred unless each of the following requirements is met:

A. ☑ The receiving facility has available space and qualified personnel for the treatment of the patient.

B. ☑ The receiving facility has agreed to ___ appropriate medical treatment.

1. Name of the receiving facility — HOSPITAL
please print

2. Name of individual accepting transfer ███████ *please print*

C. ☐ The receiving facility will be provided with appropriate medical records of the examination and treatment of the patient

D. ☑ The patient will be transferred by qualified personnel and transportation equipment as required, including the use of necessary and medical appropriate life support measures.

1. MEANS OF TRANSPORT
☑ Ground ambulance (☑ BLS ☐ ALS) _____ *name*
☐ Air ambulance (☐ BLS ☐ ALS) _____ *name*
☐ Transport Team _____ *name*
☐ Private car
☐ Other _____

2. PERSONNEL ACCOMPANYING PATIENT (check all that apply)
☐ EMT - A
☐ EMT - P
☐ Physician
☐ Nurse
☐ Respiratory Therapist
☐ Other ███

I certify that I have answered the above questions based upon the inform ___ ailable to me at the ___ of the patient's transfer. I further certif that I have made the appropriate disclosures as indicated on this form.

███████████ Name of Physician Authorizing Transfer (please print)

███████ Physician Signature

Date 3/30/01
Time 11:2_

141

HOSPITAL

RESTRAINT AND SECLUSION

Peabody,
Charlie

TO BE COMPLETED BY PHYSICIAN

REASON FOR RESTRAINT *(Check all that apply)*

☐ Self Harm / Safety Risk _____   ☐ Risk . ☐ Occurrence

☐ Harm to others/ surroundings _____   ☐ Risk ☐ Occurrence

☑ Agitation that prevents necessary examination/procedures. verbally abusive to EMTS
psychomotor agitation

TYPE OF RESTRAINT/SECLUSION   **LESS RESTRICTIVE MEASURES**
(Eg. Verbal intervention/medication)

☑ Holding Room   ☐ Secured Waiting Area   ☐ Utilized without success

☐ 4-Point   ☐ Posey   ☑ Contraindicated (i.e. immediate restraint necessary)

☐ 2-Point   ☐ Other

M.D. Signature _____   DATE 3/30/01   TIME _____

OBSERVATION LOG

HOUR	TIME :00	:15	:30	:45	TYPE OF RESTRAINTS MD SIGNATURE REVIEW EVERY 3 HOURS	TIME	BEHAVIOR
2000							
2100							Pt went to Mc Lean
2200							via Fallen Ambulance
2300							

SIGNATURE	INITIALS	SIGNATURE	INITIALS

142

Massachusetts General Hospital
Emergency Department Record

Pat: PEABODY, CHARLES   MRN: ▮▮▮   DOB: 03/21/1977   24 Years   Sex: M
Registration Date/Time: 03/30/2001 08:26 PM   ** Closed**

ED Note

Chief Complaint:	"I need to get out of here"
HPI:	24 yo SWM w h/o untreated bipolar d/o and longtime h/o refusing meds presents to APS after phoning mother reporting "I'm leaving town and you better help me you fucking bitch". Pt has been increasingly paranoid in past 2 weeks. Thinks people are following him. Spending alot of money, shopping at expensive stores. Claiming he has been communicating with celebreties. GF's father is worried pt may hurt his daughter. Mother presented to his apartment to try to convince him to come to hospital. Pt became verbally abusive and called police. When police arrived pt was found to be manic and paranoid and was brought to APS. Upon arrival pt was irritable, with pressured speach and grandiose ideas that he has "an IQ in the genius range". Wanted to know which neurotransmitter systems the medications offered were working on. Claimed he has "special abilities" to read palms and get "vibes on people's energy". Reports he was in ▮▮▮ office recently and had VH of purple lights. Otherwise denies AH/VH/IOR. Pt denies he has bipolar d/o and claims he has depression and alchohol abuse. BAL>2000 at time of admission.
PMHx:	MVA with resulting head injury w LOC x 2 days: 4-5 yrs ago.
	Asthma
	Question of "Complex Partial Sz" by EEG after MVA.
PSurHx:	Splenectomy after MVA.

Psych Hx

Hospitalization Hx:	No past psych hospitalizations.
	Mother claims pt has been "cycling since 14 yrs old" and "has been medicating with lots of drugs".
	Has h/o violent, rageful, behavior which causes fear in those around him.
	No prior SA.
Psych/PCP Treat:	▮▮▮ at McLean Hospital x 3 yrs. Pt fired him today. Pt was in outpt tx in group therapy at McLean Hosp. with "an Italian name" doctor.
	▮▮▮ for psychotherapy but therapy didn't last.
Meds:	no present meds. ▮▮▮ suggested Li or Depakote to mother.
Allergy:	No Known Drug Allergies
Family Hx:	
	Father-bipolar d/o on Neurontin and Celexa
	Grandfather- successful suicide by GSW.
	Grandmother-OD on alchohol, polysubstance abuse.
	Father's family- "all have problems with rage"

Social Hx

Employment:	Attended Univ Vermont x 1 yr, stopped after MVA.
	Lives alone in apt. funded by father. Works at ▮▮▮ in Spring and Summer as rental agent. Cannot sustain fulltime job due to affective instability.
Marital Status:	Single

PEABODY, Charles A   Admitted: 03/31/01
Medical Record No.: ██████   Unit:
Date of Birth: 03/21/1977

ADMISSION NOTE AND FIRST PERIODIC REVIEW

SOURCE OF INFORMATION: note, and the patient.

IDENTIFYING DATA AND CHIEF COMPLAINT: This is the first psychiatric hospitalization for this 24 year old man with a history of untreated bipolar I disorder who was brought in by the police for paranoia and out of control behavior. The patient states, "I'm sleeping at home tonight, and you can't stop me."

HISTORY OF PRESENT ILLNESS: Please note that most of the information in the following note is from the APS note as the patient is very disorganized and unable to provide a coherent narrative.

Apparently, over the past two weeks the patient has been increasingly paranoid, exhibiting increased spending behavior, and believes that he is communicating with celebrities. His girlfriend's father is concerned for the girlfriend's safety. Today, the patient called his mother and said, "I'm leaving town and you better help me, you bitch." She then went to his apartment to try to convince him to go to the hospital. The patient called the police, who found the patient to be agitated, paranoid and verbally abusive. They then brought him to the   for evaluation.

On arrival at   the patient was in 4-point restraints. Apparently he had become agitated when told he was to be transferred to another hospital. He was directly admitted to   . On   the patient was noted to be irritable, yelling at staff and insulting them, distractible, grandiose stating, "my 20 lawyers will get me out of here tonight," physically threatening in manner, although able to control himself, and paranoid, relating that his girlfriend's father is tapping his phone and spying on him.

PAST PSYCHIATRIC HISTORY: The patient has a long history of aggressive behavior, violent threats and anger outbursts. He has no prior psychiatric hospitalizations and no prior suicide attempts. He sees ███████████████ for the past three years and has seen ██████████ for therapy in the past. Of note, on the day of admission the patient fired ██████ in a fit of anger.

PAST MEDICAL HISTORY: Asthma, motor vehicle accident with head injury and loss of consciousness for two days, approximately 4-5 years ago.

MEDICATIONS AND COMPLIANCE: No medications.

DRUG ALLERGIES: None.

SUBSTANCE ABUSE HISTORY: The patient reports drinking alcohol about 2x a week, the amount varies. On admission he was intoxicated with an alcohol level of 2000. The patient denies all other drug use, but according to the   notes he also uses marijuana.

144

FAMILY HISTORY OF PSYCHIATRIC ILLNESS: Grandmother had problems with substance abuse. Grandfather completed a suicide by gunshot.

SOCIAL AND DEVELOPMENTAL HISTORY: The patient is currently living in the Back Bay. He is supported by his father. He completed high school. He attended the University of Vermont for one year, but had to drop out after his motor vehicle accident.

Of note, the patient was asked to leave his boarding school in his teenage years for behavioral outbursts.

The patient has worked in realty in the past, during spring and summer seasons.

LEGAL HISTORY: No formal charges.

CIVIL RIGHTS: The patient is admitted on Involuntary status.

MENTAL STATUS EXAMINATION ON ADMISSION: The patient is in hospital garments, and disheveled. Initially, he was in 4-point restraints, but these are removed. The patient remains in fair behavioral control. He is noted to be somewhat redirectable, although with a slightly threatening physical manner. He is noted to have poor balance and is stumbling somewhat in the quiet room. He makes good eye contact. He is very distractible and irritable. His speech is slurred and incoherent at times. His mood is angry. Affect is irritable. He denies suicidal and homicidal ideation. The patient exhibits grandiose delusions, and paranoid delusions. He denies auditory or visual hallucinations. His thought process is loose. Insight and judgment are poor.

INVENTORY OF ASSETS: Bright and articulate, with stable living situation, adequate financial support, and social family support.

PROVISIONAL DIAGNOSES:
Axis I: Bipolar disorder, current episode manic.
Axis II: Deferred.
Axis III: Asthma.
            Status post MVA.
Axis IV: Current life events.
Axis V: 25.

FORMULATION: This is a 24 year old man with a history of untreated bipolar disorder who presents now with out of control behavior in the setting of a two week increase in manic symptoms. Symptoms include irritability, distractibility, grandiosity, pressured speech and paranoid delusions. The patient is incoherent at times, and has obviously impaired judgment. He requires inpatient hospitalization for safety.

INITIAL TREATMENT PLAN: Admit to NB1. Estimated length of stay 7-10 days. 5 minute checks, one-to-one supervision, locked door seclusion initially, sharps and flames supervision, and hall restrict.

On the morning of September 26, 2002 at approximately 4 AM I was traveling south on ███ Road. As I passed the Myopia Polo Fields I observed the pedestrian traffic light and pole laying on the side of the road. Further investigation revealed that it had been struck by a vehicle. The light post had been severed off at the base and there were vehicle parts on the side of the road. I observed a trail of fluid (oil or antifreeze) leaving the site of the accident and traveling north on Bay Road. I followed the trail of fluid and saw that the vehicle it was dripping from had crossed over the solid double lines. Judging from the damage to the light and post I was fearful that the operator of the vehicle may have been injured. As I approached ██████ I observed the trail of fluid turn into the driveway. At this point I had followed the trail of fluid for over a mile. I continued up the driveway and found a heavily damaged green Saab sedan parked.

I exited my cruiser and checked the vehicle. There was no one inside of it. The front of the vehicle was damaged and there was yellow paint on it. The yellow paint was similar to paint on the post that had been struck. To roof of the vehicle had a large crease down the center of it and the back window had been broken. The crease had been caused by the signal post falling back onto the car after it had been knocked from it's base. I had control run a listing on the vehicle's license plate and found it to be registered to Charles A Peabody III of Boston. At this time I was joined by Officer ██████ and went to the residence at ██████

After ringing the bell for several minutes I was greated by ██████ who resides at that address. I told her we were investigating an accident and asked if Mr. Peabody was there. She stated that he was and that he had come home around 2 AM. She further stated that she knew he had been in an accident. I informed her that I would like to speak to Mr. Peabody. After checking several rooms in the large home she found him in the kitchen sleeping. Mr. Peabody came out of the kitchen and into the hall. He was drinking a soda. He seemed to be intoxicated , his eyes were glassy, his speech slurred, and his balance unsteady. I detected an odor of liquor on his breath and his appearance was very disheveled. I asked if he had been in an accident and he stated that he had been. I asked how long ago the accident had occured and he stated an hour or longer and that he had been sleeping for a while at the ██████ I asked what had happened and he said he left the roadway while looking for his wallet and struck something. I asked why he left the scene of the accident. He did not give a clear answer. I asked again why he did not report the accident, and he said in slurred speech " I was going to in the morning, and get a tow truck for the car " At this time ██████ daughter was also in the hall with us and stated that Mr. Peabody was her boyfriend. Both ██████ and her daughter said that Mr. Peabody had returned home around 2 AM. When asked for his license Mr. Peabody replied I'll go get it then fumbled around in his rear pocket and produced his wallet. He had difficulty pulling the licence from his wallet. I explained to Mr. Peabody that he would be charged with leaving the scene of a property damage accident and possibly other motor vehicle offenses after I finished the accident report. I further explained to Mr. Peabody that I would mail the citation to his address or he could pick it up at the police station. Mr. Peabody started to ramble on in slurred speach about how he pays over $3,000.00 a year for car insurance.

After leaving the ██████ I returned to the scene of the accident. I took several measurements and notified the State Highway Dept of the damaged signal. The light post had several uncovered electric wires coming out of the stump. The Highway Dept responded immediately. After returning to the station I completed an accident report, filled out a citation and placed it with the out going mail.

Crash Diagram:

Bay Road

Traffic light and post

If Crash Did Not Occur on a Public Way:

☐ Off-Street Parking Lot

☐ Garage

☐ Mall/Shopping Center

☐ Other Private Way

North

Crash Narrative:

The operator left the roadway traveled approximately 40' and struck a traffic light pole. He then returned to the roadway and left the area. He was cited for leaving the scene of a property damage accident and marked lanes.

Witnesses:

Name (Last,First,Middle)	Address	Phone #	Statement

Property Damage:

Owner (Last,First,Middle)	Address	Phone #	34-Type	Description of Damaged Property
COMMONWEALTH OF MA.	HIGHWAY DEPT. IPSWICH MA 01938			TRAFFIC LIGHT AND POST

Truck and Bus Information.

Registration # _____ (From Vehicle Section)

Carrier Name _____ Carrier Issuing Authority Code [35]

Address _____ City _____ St _____ Zip _____

US DOT #: _____ State Number _____ Issuing State _____ ICC #: _____ Interstate [36]

Cargo Body Type Code [37]   Gross Vehicle Weight [38]

Trailer Reg #: _____ Reg Type _____ Reg State _____ Reg Year _____ Trailer Length [39]

Hazmat Information:

Placard [40]   Material 1 digit # [41]   Material Name _____ Material 4 digit # _____ Release code [42]

Sergeant ▬▬▬▬▬

Police Officer Name (Please Print)   Signature   ID/Badge #   Department

Police Department   09/26/2002

Precinct/Barracks   Date

CDP1 11-14-00

147

8

THE PROCESS OF GETTING BETTER

It was six days and counting up North. Getting a little itchy. My issue was a $20,000 bonus waiting for me back at the dump of a real estate office I worked at. Returning meant bonus for Charlie; staying meant no bonus *and* no more job. The money had a ribbon and bow around it in my head, but the head can be a dangerous place to unwrap gifts. I somehow believed that I wouldn't be okay without that money. I thought that life would never return to normalcy unless I had my hands on it. But was it money I needed? No. I was on the precipice of change and terrified of being happy. Perfect time to tackle a 2nd Step.

"So Charlie, what do you think of when you think of God?"

Simple enough question. For north shore Episcopalians, God and religion amounted to Easter Sunday, Christmas Eve carols, and a few Christenings sprinkled here and there. We were social Christians. We didn't go to church. We didn't talk about God. We didn't praise

Jesus. To be perfectly honest, we did nothing other than remain complacently agnostic like most alcoholics and drug addicts.

Well, maybe there is, maybe there isn't, but if there is, God hasn't done shit for me. Wait! Put me down for a 'yes', just in case.

When I heard the word 'God', I thought of church steeples, pipe organs, nutbag fundamentalists, the Inquisition, the Bible, Jah Rastafari, and other doctrines, codes and creeds floating around. To me, God was reduced to a social construct. Sitting in church was the last place I felt the presence of God. I felt it out in the woods, near the ocean, playing music, or feeling love for someone. Religion was impersonal. There was no active internal experience, and I needed something real. Okay, next question.

"Do you believe any of those things will cure your alcoholism and drug addiction?"

"Nope. I'm pretty sure a building can't fix me."

"But can even you fix you?"

No answer.

I always figured that if I was ever going to get better, it was Charlie who would do it. In fact, I attributed every accomplishment or good thing I did to me and me only. But I suppose the guy had a point.

I was sitting there in rehab wearing four shirts in the middle of July, and I didn't exactly have the best track record. Why not trust in something other than myself? Plus, if I can believe that my alcoholism and heroin addiction are greater than me, why can't I believe that there's something else greater than me that can get me better? And who am I to say there is no God? Who am I, the all-knowing?

Faith would mean putting aside my passion for illuminating the phony in others. I had the tendency to accost apocalyptic Jesus freaks on the streets of Boston. They stood in the subway stations wearing double-sided wooden planks around their necks, passing out cartoon pamphlets about the end of the world. How dare they tell me I don't know the truth? I burned to convince them that much of their brain was void of anything useful, such as intellect.

I loved my brain. I loved my intellect. I craved for others to feel dumb. I wore around a cloak of intellectual superiority and for years my only skill set of consequence was verbal abuse. But it's pretty cocky to believe that over 90% of the world's population, all who had faith in some Higher Power, were wrong. Six billion people don't have a clue, but I do? Not to mention the millions of religious people that work hard, love their families, do the right thing, and guess what? They don't have to sniff heroin all day long or get plastered to refrain from complaining incessantly. Who am I to judge them anyway? I'm a junkie. I need to sniff 80 milligrams of OxyContin just to have a two-minute conversation with my wife.

"Charlie, this process is asking you to take a leap of faith here, to step into the darkness, unsure of where you will land. Why not go to any lengths to get better?"

Translation: If I give my whole self to this program, I will not fail. For the first time in my life, I was to trust in something other than my narcissistic extensions. I was to give myself away to God and to certain spiritual principles with nothing but sheer trust that I'd be okay. This is what it meant to *really* let go. I couldn't allow the delusion of human pride to stop me from recovering.

Quite frankly, any life can hardly be fulfilling driven by self-will. Sure, plowing through this way I may accomplish anything and everything in the world, but I'll starve from the most important thing - peace. Who cares what I have or what I'm doing if I feel like shit inside? And the truth is that all I ever wanted was just to be okay once the substances and distractions were removed.

A few months before going to detox, I showed up at Mom's house in Cambridge. It was late spring. I pulled into her driveway and got out of my car, proud as a king for showing up to help her with something. As she walked out of the door, all I remember was her jaw dropping. She gasped and stared at me in shock. Running over to take a closer look, she began.

"Charlie, Oh my God! You're so thin. What's happening to you? What's wrong? Are you eating?"

The way she looked at me was frightening. I perked up at once.

"No, no, you've got it all wrong. I'm great. See? Look at those muscles! I've been working out. I'm just super fit and eating mostly vegetarian."

Not exactly sure what bullshit I fed her afterwards, but it was useless anyway. I don't know if it was that day or the next when I caved.

"I'm having a problem with painkillers…"

I didn't have the heart to tell her it was OxyContin, heroin, cocaine, Methadone, benzodiazepines, etc. etc. I knew she'd find out later in the toxicology report, so why not spare her the heartache and myself the shame for a day or two.

But Mom, as usual, looked at me lovingly.

"What can I do? I'll do anything. We'll do anything. What's it gonna' take? You name it, any doctor, treatment, medication, rehab, anything. There must be something I can do!"

Back then I didn't know how to tell Mom that there was absolutely nothing neither she nor anyone else could do. There was nothing I could take, nothing I could learn, nothing that could be beaten into me, nothing that all the money in the world could buy that would cure me. My problem wasn't even really drugs and booze, but what happened to me in their absence. The truth? I was missing something, and it was now time to fill up the abyss. It was time to rely on something other than my fucked up head to guide me through life. It was time to evolve and to learn how to pray.

So I took a 3rd Step. I wrote it out on a piece of paper to make sure I did it perfectly, and then met some fellow junkies in the chapel. I brought a pillow for my bony knees because I was still a little wimp. We knelt down and held hands. Sadness overcame me and I began crying as we recited the prayer together.

"God, I offer myself to Thee - to build with me and do with me as Thou wilt. Relieve me of the bondage of self, that I may better do Thy will. Take away my difficulties, that victory over them may bear witness to those I would help of Thy Power, Thy Love, and Thy Way of life. May I do Thy will always!" *Alcoholics Anonymous, 63.*

Nothing happened. All I got were some instructions on writing inventory. And since belief alone is not enough, action was just what I needed.

Up North, they write inventory. 4th Step written inventory encompasses an entire lifetime of individual resentments, fears, and sexual misconduct. Contained within these categories is every ounce of spiritual poison that sits inside me, feeding my addiction and depression. It is the mountain of filth that brought me down, shattered my spirit, twisted my moral compass, shrunk my conscience, burned bridges, and broke the hearts of many.

Inventory is a life exorcism - a housecleaning of the broken mind. The task was to unearth all things that shame me to the core, including every skeleton in the closest, every hidden immoral, selfish, cruel or criminal act; things I've buried away, intending to haul to my grave.

"This is your chance to recover, Charlie, so be thorough and fearless. If not, you will surely relapse."

"What if I can't remember everything?"

"Oh, you will. But if not, then pray and it'll come out of you like a snake."

"I have so many stupid, petty resentments. Should I cut some out?"

"The more the better. Think of each one as a chance. The pettiest resentment may be the one that saves your life."

Difference between this and say, 25 years of psychotherapy, is a) it doesn't take 25 years, and b) I take full responsibility for everything inside me. This is necessary because I have caused all resentment single-handedly. Nothing external is to blame, and therefore I own it. I give birth to resentment by choosing to see events as acting upon me rather than attracting the events to myself. Then it grows worse by choosing to react to events that I falsely believe something else is responsible for. This is how narcissism gets out of hand.

Charlie feeling good was dependent on the world around him, what other people said or did, the moods of my wife or family members. When Wife is in a bad mood, I'm not okay. I resent her for being in pain because it takes me out of my comfort zone. Pretty selfish, huh? I'll even hold social stratification or environmental degradation responsible for my feelings. Letting go of my emotional dependence on the external world = internal freedom. Anger and resentment born within and left alone to brood will kill me. It is a poison that will crush an addict's mind and soul no sooner than heroin itself. Worst of all, it pushes me away from God.

The whole process was rigorous and painstaking. It's written in a column format. The instructions were: a) write the names of every *person, institution,* and *principle* I've ever resented, b) write *each specific resentment* for each person, institution and principle, c) write how each specific resentment affected me in terms of my *self-esteem, pride* or *ambition, personal* or *sex relationships,* sense of *security,* or *my wallet,* and d) then the actual work begins. The last column asks me to discover how I was a) *self-seeking b) selfish c) dishonest,* and d) *fearful* in each one of the resentments.

Remembering that resentments have nothing to do with the other person, place, or principle, I ask myself some questions: What did I do to give birth to the resentment? How was I trying to be seen by others? How was I trying to see myself? How was I being selfish? What did I want? What was I trying to keep or protect? What was I unable to see? How am I to blame? Do I do the very thing that I resent? Was I not honest with my feelings? What was I afraid of?

Here's an example:

1st Column - Name Mom
2nd Column - Resentment a. Thinks I should be medicated.
3rd Column - Affects my… SE (self-esteem) P/A (pride/ambition) P/SR (personal/sex relations)
4th Column - Mistaken thinking *Self-seeking: I wanted to be seen as normal and sane. *Selfish: I wanted to be left alone (because it felt uncomfortable). I was unable to see that Mom was just trying to help me. *Dishonest: I knew I was sick (but getting angry at Mom helped me avoid taking responsibility). *Fear: I feared what others thought of me. I feared facing my depression.

Skeptics like to argue with me and say that it's never our own fault when someone, for example, sexually or physically abuses us as a child. Of course an abuser's actions towards me are not my fault. But how I choose to react to that event is most certainly my fault. If I take that anger and unleash it onto the world around me for years to come, that is my fault, that is wrong, and that is selfish. There is no getting better unless I discover my own fault in these resentments.

Anger and resentment are like acid to a seeing eye. They burn and blind the eye so that it cannot see clearly anymore. As long as they inhabit the body, forgiveness is impossible. But when I become accountable for everything in my life, all of it magically crumbles and suddenly I can forgive anyone. I just don't care anymore because there is nothing left to blame. Above all, I can forgive myself. That is a miracle.

I wrote seven to eight hours a day for thirteen days, breaking through layer upon layer of bullshit. Sometimes it was illegible. Sometimes my pen went through the paper. Sometimes it felt like a never-ending mountain towering before me. Soon I was hauling around a stack of notebooks, filled front to back and stuffed to the brim with the crap that delivered me to heroin.

And then a single comment from a staffer one night pissed me off so much that I went upstairs and packed my bags. I was ready to hurl away every bit of work I had accomplished like it was garbage.

It was nighttime. I sat outside writing away, cigarettes to my right, asthma medicine to my left.

"Hey Charlie, how you doin' with all this? Gee… it looks like you're writing a lot for each answer. You know, writing too much might lead to backtracking. With this stuff it's like 99% = zero. Know what I mean?"

Zero? What I've just done for eight hours a day is fucking zero? My heart sank. I tried to repress it but I was livid. Rage boiled up inside. I was so proud of what I'd done. And when my ego is stabbed, I'm hard-wired to retaliate by sabotaging myself. I somehow think that I'm getting back at people by screwing myself. I fumed about it all night long. Set to leave the next morning against staff recommendation, I called Wife with my new agenda.

"Sweetheart, this treatment center is just a physical location. I can finish writing anywhere. I have what I need now. That's the point, right?"

She didn't fall for it. I was on the precipice and wanted to step back. Or turn around altogether. I knew this was it. I went outside, looked up, and saw a Red-Tailed hawk circling above. Among certain Native American traditions, the hawk is seen as a messenger, and so one must either beware or be aware, especially if there is an opportunity to be grabbed. That moment may have been my last great chance to act with courage, to embrace this once in a lifetime opportunity.

So I stayed. And having done the more difficult thing, I suddenly felt lighter. I felt a growing absence of fear. I was growing up. I was getting stronger. Something magical was about to happen.

But first, there was more inventory. Fear inventory. The instructions were: a) write down each *fear* I've ever had, b) write *why* I fear each one c) dig deeper to find *why I really* fear each one, and d) figure out *why it's selfish* to have that fear. The basic task was to peel away and uncover what was really underneath my fears.

Here are a few examples:

1st Column – Fear
Spiders
2nd Column – Why do I fear this?
They freak me out.
3rd Column – Why do I *really* fear this?
They make me act like a wimp.
4th Column – How is this fear selfish?
I kill them so I don't have to feel uncomfortable.

1st Column – Fear
Public speaking
2nd Column – Why do I fear this?
It makes me self-conscious.
3rd Column – Why do I *really* fear this?
I have to step outside my comfort zone.
4th Column – How is this fear selfish?
I refuse to speak publically even though it may help others.

1st Column – Fear
Becoming Dad

2nd Column – Why do I fear this?
I'm prone to depression.

3rd Column – Why do I *really* fear this?
I fear what others think of me.

4th Column – How is this fear selfish?
Time spent thinking about this is time I'm not spending helping and loving Dad.

Fear is selfish. It prevents me from being useful and from growing spiritually. I thought it was real and that feelings might actually kill me. But by avoiding things that scared me, the fear grew stronger. So to deflate it, I just do the exact thing that frightens me. If I fear confrontation, I confront. If I fear public speaking, I speak publically. If I fear intimacy, I become intimate. To conquer it, do it. Doing it vaporizes the fear and gradually the action in question becomes easier. Someone told me once that I don't have to let feelings stop me. Guess I managed to block that out for a while.

After four and a half notebooks, I really wanted to be done. Nope. More work. Sex inventory. The instructions were: a) write *who*

I've hurt, b) write *who else I've hurt*, c) write *what happened*, and d) write *what I should have done* instead.

Here's an example:

1st Column - Who? College girl
2nd Column - Who else? Her husband
3rd Column - What happened? Slept with her knowing she was married, and pretended I cared about her.
4th Column - What should I have done instead? Left her alone. At the very least I should have masturbated rather than destroy someone's marriage.

As a conscienceless addict, I filled my emptiness by manipulating women and using them for sex. I used a foreign girl in college fully aware that she was married. I used my gifts to manipulate her, taking her into piano rooms on campus and playing Chopin while I stared into her eyes. From piano recitals to piano room seductions... this is what I became. I acted like I cared about women just to have sex with them, and then I got as far away as possible. I showed little or no remorse at all. And when I showed it, I never really felt it inside. Yes, I knew it was wrong, but satisfying lust was far more important. That's the sort of behavior that must cease forever if I plan on staying sober.

That concluded my 4th Step inventory. It's one of the hardest things I've ever done. I pulled my hair out trying to get honest about every single thing in my life. I consider it to be one of my greatest accomplishments.

The 5th Step instructed me to read ALL of it to another person. Why do this? For one, it's humbling and nauseating. It also ensures that I don't get off the hook with anything, an unfortunate leniency always afforded me in therapy. That's not going to work anymore. Everything came pouring out. I read for eleven and a half hours in the little chapel up North.

The 6th Step was a *one-hour meditation* on becoming ready to have my demented personality removed. Left alone, there I was in the chapel, beams of moonlight shining down through the skylights. I stood in the middle of the room trying to meditate, following my breath in my mind, "*In… Out… In… Out…*" Suddenly my thoughts went on autopilot as I ran through all the negative patterns revealed from my inventory.

Given that I've wanted to be seen as strong, secure, smart, beautiful, heroic, tough, normal... Given that I've been selfish by remaining in my comfort zone, always protecting my pride, ego, self-esteem... Given that I have failed to see how I affected others... Given that I do the very things I resent in others - being fake, arrogant, self-absorbed... Given that I've been scared to grow up and be responsible, accountable... Given that I've been unwilling to change and push through hard times... Given I've been this way and that way...

Then I reached out from within.

"God, I humbly ask you to remove these shortcomings... and replace them with Love."

Exactly one hour passed. No clocks, no watch, no time keeping, nothing. Here's where it gets mystical. What happened next, I cannot with any justice describe in words. But let me try.

"God, help me to see those things
that block me from You and Others"

Mom | a. Thinks I should be medicated | SE
P/A
P/SR

Mom a. ⊗ Self-Seeking: I am perfectly fucking
normal.

⊗ Selfish: Unable to see that Mom just wants
me to be happy and doesn't know
any other way to help.

⊗ Dishonest: I pretty much know I'm sick
and depressed, but I get angry at Mom
to cover it up and avoid taking responsibility

⊗ Fear: I fear getting better, I fear
Others thinking I'm sick and weak

167

9

HAND OF GOD

It was the middle of a moonlit night in the chapel up North. My body told me when I was finished meditating. I sat down for a few minutes. A feeling of certainty calmed me. I was ready. I knelt down on my knees and opened up the Big Book of Alcoholics Anonymous to page 76 and read the 7th Step prayer out loud.

"My Creator, I am now willing that you should have all of me, good and bad. I pray that you now remove from me every single defect of character which stands in the way of my usefulness to you and my fellows. Grant me strength, as I go out from here, to do your bidding. Amen." *Alcoholics Anonymous, 76.*

As I finished reading the prayer, an unexplainable miracle occurred. The instant I was done, something rushed through my body. Something wonderful. I laughed and cried simultaneously. It was strange. Some force immediately took over my body and mind, controlling me for some time. Then a volcanic feeling of relief and rapture pervaded my entire being. I remember thinking, *Holy shit. It worked!* I felt it in every cell.

I stood up and walked into the main room. I felt as light as air. From somewhere up in the Universe came a rush of energy. At first it was a surge... then a steady flow of God rushed through me, entering through the top of my head and flowing down through my feet and back out. I was emptied out. My mind was clear for the first time in my life. Totally, utterly, empty.

Then a second miracle occurred. I suddenly had full control over my mind. I could choose to think or not to think, but I had the choice. It was pure and absolute freedom. A telephone line had been activated between me and God, and in that moment I knew with certainty that I could tap into this Universal Power at any time. I realized that I had just tapped into Power.

Then a third miracle occurred as I experienced a total absence of fear. All fear just gone. It was unbelievable. Deep inside, I knew I would be okay from that point on. There was nothing fear could ever again stop me from doing. There was no problem anymore. Something had shifted. For the next several days, I entered a prolonged state of calm and inner peace. I was reborn - no religiosity intended. Since those moments up North, I've felt exponentially better than I ever did high on drugs or alcohol.

What occurred that night was an intense spiritual experience. The mental obsession was lifted from my broken mind. Before, my shoulders were hunched over from the heavy load of resentments and grief that I carried around with me. But suddenly, I stood straight up, shoulders cocked backed, eyes and face aglow. A limitless and mind-blowing power brushed me for a brief moment. And so I was restored to sanity.

I was touched by the hand of God that night and it was no hallucination. No human thing is responsible for what I felt, for what flowed into me, for what changed me. I refuse to take any responsibility for what happened and I am so grateful and humbled by that. From then on, I have been willing to do anything it takes to get better, to stay better, and to grow spiritually.

I walked out of the chapel and entered what felt like a different realm. Fog hovered over the grass, deflecting beams of light in every direction. Everything was vibrant. The earth was breathing. I was alive. Away I went to fall sound asleep.

In the morning, something was fundamentally different. I needed less and didn't think about myself as much. I wanted to help others and be useful. I wanted other people to have what I had.

People noticed what happened. No one could not ignore it. The change in the way I looked and in my mental state and attitude could not be mistaken. And it happened to all of us who sought out a spiritual experience. We were taken over and glowing from Spirit within. Truly amazing.

August 17, 2005

To Whom It May Concern:

The purpose of this letter is to certify that Charles Peabody was a guest at our facility from 07/27/05 through 08/17/05 and was discharged in good standing. Charles demonstrated a strong commitment to sobriety performed all suggested work via the 12-Step Recovery Program.

The ▓▓▓▓▓▓▓ schedule is a grueling one; beginning at 8 A.M. and ending at 10 P.M. daily, there are 43 mandatory groups and workshops weekly, and numerous optional seminars and meetings. Charles participated in all mandatory and optional groups.

Should you have any questions about Charles or the ▓▓▓ ▓▓▓, please feel free to call us at any time at ▓▓▓▓▓

Sincerely,

Discharge Summary

Guest Name: Charles Peabody

Admit Date: 7/27/2005   Discharge Date: 8/17/2005

Presenting Problem: Opiate Dep.

A recovery center dedicated to teaching the life-changing principles of the Twelve-Step Program.

1. Program Resume

   A. Program Participation

      ☑ Guest compliant, punctual with program activities/rules.

      ☑ Guest cooperative, positive in interactions with other guest and staff.

   B. Acceptance of Program Principles

      ☑ Guest exhibits an awareness and acceptance of addiction and commitment to self-directed recovery plan.

      ☑ Guest able to recognize severity of use.

      ☑ Guest verbalizing life problems related to addiction.

      ☑ Guest verbalizing initial concepts of spirituality.

      ☑ Guest applying skills necessary to maintain sobriety.

   C. Commitment to Continuing Car

      ☑ Guest verbalizing specific continuing care recovery plan..

   D. Social/Family Status

      ☑ Guest developed coping skills to deal with current living environment.

2. Services Provided

      ☑ Daily Reflection's Meeting

      ☑ Big Book Meeting daily

      ☑ Weekly men's/women's meeting

      ☑ Daily Chapel

      ☑ Nightly recovery meeting

      ☑ Fourth Step Workshop (optional)

      ☑ AA Literature Meeting

      ☑ Individual counsling (optional)

      ☑ Aftercare Planning

10

BOYS FROM THE MEN

I met my new sponsor the day after I returned home. He looked at me and smiled.

"You need to make amends. And don't forget to keep writing inventory. And pray before you do anything!"

Great… more work.

A few days later, just before a local AA meeting, I was accosted by some AA guy while trying to purchase ice coffee at Dunkin Donuts. His idea of helping me was pulling me out of line and mindlessly asserting that it was "way too early" to make amends.

"You won't be ready to do that for like years, bro."

"Years? I won't make it that long just getting 'ready'… bro."

How dangerous it was to digest that sort of advice, though nonetheless a common approach to sponsorship in my region. I looked at him for a while. I didn't want anything he had. I wasn't interested in holding on by a thread, day after day. I wasn't interested in suffering anymore. I looked him in the eye.

"It's never too early to get better."

Several days later, I woke up with a feeling in my gut that couldn't be ignored. An old boss of mine would not get out of my head. I knew what I had to do and with no delay. A nervous energy crawled around my skin. Knots tightened up in my stomach. But something else was driving me now. There was no walking away. Hell, I would have suffered more by avoiding it. Neglecting the people I have harmed would sever my cord to God.

I got in my car and drove to a nearby town. The moving company I worked for years ago had a large, wide-open, dirt yard in front of the office. Parking was located on the far side, opposite the office. No getting around it, I was in for the prolonged and agonizing walk of shame across the yard to my old boss's office. For years, I drove right by the place, but driving by wasn't a choice anymore. I am now contracted to go to any lengths to recover. I had to see my old boss or I'd eventually relapse.

My heart pounded as I got out of my car, sweating and shaking like an animal wrought with fear. I walked across the long dirt yard in the blazing sun. It was hot. Fear leaked out through my pores. It felt like an eternity. *What the hell am I doing?*

I made it. Then I patted myself on the back for having come this far. My old boss... wasn't there. Imagine that. His secretary told me that he'd be back in an hour. I left and drove down the street to a nearby train station parking lot to wait out the hour. All I could do was sit in my car, chain-smoke cigarettes, and let the ceaseless anticipation make me nervous as hell. I rehearsed what I had to say and then prayed over and over and over. Soon it was just, "God, be with me. God, be with me. God, be with me." I said it out loud, fast and repeatedly. It wasn't long before my t-shirt and boxers were completely soaked. *Fantastic... I'm sweating through the ass of my pants.*

An hour later, I drove back to the yard and again took the walk of shame. I was going to make this fucking amends and get it over with. There she was again... and no boss.

"Oh, just another fifteen minutes or so."

I went back to the train station. More fear, more praying, more sweat, more cigarettes.

A third time, I went back and saw his truck. A third time, I walked across the yard of agony. It was as if God had laid down my own field of humility. As I entered the office, he looked up sternly from his chair.

"What do you got?" sharply, defensive.

"Can we talk for a couple minutes?"

"Uh… yeah, I guess so. Let's go outside."

He got up and followed me outside the office. Unfortunately, I was in no condition for coherency. We stood looking out over the dried-up yard. I could barely form a sentence, let alone a thought.

Then Power suddenly came and spoke through me. "I came to be accountable for the fact that I wronged you. When I worked here, I was selfish. I was an active drug addict. I sold drugs to your employees. I betrayed your trust by driving around high in company trucks with your clients' valuable possessions, things I may have smashed up while driving around like an idiot. I stole pills from people's houses. I put your reputation and your employees at risk with the way I acted… and that was wrong.

I should've been grateful for the job you gave me. You've always been good to my family. Worst of all was that ridiculous threat-letter I wrote demanding $5,000, all because I was pissed off when you sent me out on a long-distance job and wasn't at the office when I got back late at night. It was my stupid plan to keep getting high all day without having to work. I was ashamed and avoided you ever since, and that is wrong of me. So… is there anything I can do to make it right?"

"Wow. No. I really appreciate you comin' down here and saying that. You're, like, a man now. Just let me know if there's anything I can do for you."

The guy wants to help me out after what I did to him. That's the magic of humility. Fine, so the amends weren't as bad as my narcissistic, alcoholic self predicts they will be. I began realizing that my grandiosity was a figment of my imagination, that other people aren't permanently infatuated with my life. *So you mean people don't spend all day long thinking about me?*

A few days after that, I went to confront an entire north shore police department. I owed at least some representative of the local force an amends for eating twelve Klonopin, passing out at the wheel, destroying public property, endangering lives, and mouthing off to the responding officer.

I drove towards the police station and wimped out. I sped right by, pulled over, and turned around. I drove by again. I pulled over and turned around again. Sped right by. Back and forth, I drove by maybe ten, fifteen times. I finally got paranoid that they'd think I was some madman and come pull me over, so I drove in and self-consciously got out of my car.

No policemen were immediately available. I hesitated and allowed the nervous anticipation to grow. I could feel narrow streams of sweat dripping down from my pits along the backside of my arm. I had to bang on the glass loudly to get their attention. An officer finally came around and asked me what I wanted.

"Uh... I just had to come in here and be accountable for the fact that I wronged an officer years ago and put the whole town at risk. I was the jerk who uprooted the traffic pole on Rt. 1A, left the scene of the accident, and mouthed off to the responder. I was selfish, I could have killed people, I took no responsibility... and I was cocky. I had to come in and say that what I did was wrong. I'm a drug addict and my mind was warped then, but it's different now. I'd be happy to do some community service or something. Is there anything I can..."

"You just did." the officer interrupted. "Thanks for coming in and good luck with everything. Keep it up."

And that was that.

One day in Cambridge, I was running some errands with Mom. We pulled over at some random store to buy cigarettes. I walked in and saw a girl on my amends list that I hadn't seen in ten years. There she was standing right in front of me. I believe God put her in my path. Bumping into her serendipitously was a chance laid out for me to get better. Up North, I was told to jump on those chances. Ignoring them will only cause me pain, not to mention the people I owe the amends to. I sought out every person on my list and prayed to bump into those I couldn't find.

Several days later, I awoke torn inside. I knew exactly what the doctor ordered. It was an old friend. I drove him to the airport one day with the simple task of returning the other passenger back home - his girlfriend. But that wouldn't do. I picked up a case of Harpoon, took her back to my house, and had some fun with her body. That's the kind of friend I was. I ruined their relationship and broke his heart. Too ashamed, I never took responsibility for what I did. Now I had to drive up to his front door, admit my wrong, and let him say what he never had the chance to say nine years ago.

I drove around in circles once I got to his neighborhood. Stupid, really, because I knew I wasn't leaving until the deed was done. So eventually I pulled over, walked up to the door, and knocked. No answer. I knocked again and again. Finally, his mother answered and went to fetch him. I heard her explaining that Charlie Peabody was at the front door and wished to speak.

All I heard then was some very firm resolve. "I don't wanna' fuckin' talk to him."

He had no desire to entertain me, and I don't blame him one bit. He wouldn't even come to the door. Embarrassment bit me all over as the guilt began to weigh me down.

I felt tired driving away. And then it hit me how deeply I had hurt my old friend. Maybe I scarred him. I drove down the narrow, windy streets of Cape Ann and felt a profound sadness. At least I was able to speak to this mother before leaving and tried to somehow make the amends through her. She told me to come back a few weeks later, which I did, but again he didn't answer. I shoved a letter under the door. It was all I could do. Months passed.

A couple months later, I got a phone message from him. He forgave me and was glad that I was living right. It was a wonderful moment when I heard his voice on my cell phone. I felt the presence of God in that fleeting moment. I realized that these sorts of actions change the world.

But what about my wife and family? They have no interest in a few brief remarks of regret and then I wipe my hands and off I go. Nope. They deserve that I change and act right each and every day until I die. And the people in their lives deserve that I change. By constantly worrying Mom sick, I robbed her boyfriend of having a full relationship with her. I made an amends to him and others wounded by the ripple effect of my behavior. Constant effort is the right thing to do. Besides, they may need to spill their pain months or years from now. I don't get to dictate when they get their time on stage.

Up North, the wise ones were crystal clear. "Having the courage to make these amends versus walking away to remain in your comfort zone is what separates the boys from the men and the girls from the women in this process."

That's all I needed to hear. No one tells me I'm not a man. For fifteen years, I walked around difficulty and now it was time to walk through it. Facing the people I hurt was so powerful that it fundamentally changed me as a person. I began treating people with greater love and acceptance. I was becoming sane again. Any addict can get sober, but to fix insanity, he must change the way he thinks, speaks, and acts.

None of this I did perfectly, of course. Flying high on my new spiritual buzz, I made several tactless maneuvers. I came home and thought I was going to completely change mainstream AA and re-educate everybody. I saw myself as a healer and I was going to heal the people.

I was also going to heal the woman that my wife and I sat listening to in an AA meeting one day. She was one year sober and still suffering horrendously from the thoughts in her mind. Unfortunately, I wimped out and never raised my hand to speak. Even more unfortunate was that Wife recognized her as a waitress who worked at a local restaurant. So being the idiot that I was, I called the restaurant impulsively and introduced myself as the stranger from the AA meeting. I went on to tell her about a meditation technique that I learned up North and how it will save her life… and she, uh, thought I was a psychopathic stalker.

A couple weeks later, I was cornered and accosted at another meeting by a gang of untreated alcoholism. They thought I was some sicko who enjoyed stalking women twice my age.

"If you come near our AA women, why, we'll beat the daylights outa' ya'!"

"Listen guys, I assure you that my intentions were sincere. Obviously, I went about it the wrong way, but I was just trying to help her."

I attempted to explain, but was no match for insanity. But I was the one who created this whole mess with my ridiculous approach. So sure I tried too hard at first, but eventually mistakes became lessons - to accept myself, to trust in my recovery, to step back and not push so hard. I was learning how to let go, in everyday life.

Forget those crazy local meetings. I took over a 'Chapter 2' AA meeting in Boston. Chapter 2 AA meetings embrace a rare format committed to pulling the Twelve Steps directly out of the Big Book. Chapter 2 in the Big Book is appropriately entitled, *There is a Solution*. There is no hierarchy or rules against newcomers. New people can speak and even ask questions. We don't strangle you if you double dip. We don't remove your chair if you don't laugh at our jokes. There are no coffee and cookies. There are no chips or hot dogs or sober dancing. There is no smoke break, sobriety coins, or sob stories. There is no self-pity or attention given to personal problems. It's not group therapy or social hour. It's not even about the meeting. We are there to unveil a solution for alcoholism and drug addiction in hopes that anyone suffering will become inspired to actually go do the work involved in the Steps and perhaps establish an appropriate relationship with God.

Public reaction was more than skeptical. People came in, sat down, listened for two minutes, and then barged out of the meeting, totally enraged by the format. Older folks were infuriated that someone my age had the audacity to challenge their program of recovery.

My first night, some guy rolled in and couldn't contain himself.

"What the hell kind of format is this? Why are *you* the only one reading?! Who the hell are you anyway?"

"I'm Charlie."

"Charlie! Who the hell is Charlie? I want to read! Let me read!"

He starts reading out loud and then stops.

"Who says *you* can lead the group?!" now red in the face and frothing at the mouth. I thought the poor chap might have an aneurism.

"I was asked to take this group over by the guy who ran it prior. I'm leading the group because I'm qualified to break down this process from actual experience. When you take Steps, I'll let you read."

It was tough. People stormed out left and right, huffing and puffing, making comments under their breath. I suppose they were deeply offended about the notion of doing some real work on themselves. There were some regulars though - a woman who prepared entrees during the first half and ate them during the second half, an older gentlemen who hated the Big Book and came to argue it or engage in other philosophical debates, and students from a graduate program sent to observe alcoholics in their natural habitat. The students were, by far, the most astute.

"Why do you think you're a victim of alcoholism when you're the one screwing yourself up, when you're the one being selfish? Why do alcoholics refuse to take responsibility for their actions?"

Finally someone who gets it!

I think my favorite was the hardcore AA guy who had it all figured out. He came in with his sponsee glued to his hip.

"Hey kid, you leadin' this group?"

"Uh-huh."

"Well, where's the freakin' coffee at? What kind of AA meeting doesn't have coffee or cookies?"

"A good one. We focus on getting better here, not on eating. Coffee's down the street at Dunkin' Donuts. And call my mom' if you want some cookies."

That didn't go over too well.

"How much clean time you got, kid?"

"Six months."

"Yeah, I figured. You're unqualified to chair a meeting. I got twelve years, big guy."

Funny thing is, I wanted nothing he had.

"Good for you, but recovery isn't a function of time. Recovery is a function of the actions you take to grow, and at what frequency you take them."

I know people only six months into recovery who I trust with my life because I know what they've done. I know they are willing to go to any lengths to get better. They are fully aware that being sane depends on being honest. Truth be told, they are far more centered, coherent, and at peace with themselves than the sober but untreated alcoholism that came into my Brookline Chapter 2 meeting. My friends in this process are a joy to be in the company of because they don't dump their woes on me, which is nice because then I don't end up with a migraine after a five-minute, one-sided conversation.

In neutral position, I naturally flow backwards. That means if I don't continue to move forward, I get sicker. I guess I'm just screwed up that way. As soon as I think that I'm finally okay, a million things piss me off. I had to keep writing inventory about every little petty thing that annoyed me – a kid with his hat on sideways and pants ten sizes too big that hung a foot below his ass, a girl wearing sunglasses the size of her face, a rich trust-baby on her cell phone tailing me in the car Daddy bought, a north shore snob pulling into a handicapped parking space, or a meathead cutting me off in his Infiniti. You name it, I resent it. So I wrote, prayed, and meditated as much I as could stand.

Then six months into recovery, I came flying off the pink cloud I was perched upon. I don't know why, but suddenly I came crashing down emotionally. It was the makings of a depression and I was absolutely terrified. I mean, I thought I was okay... so what's all this about? I had a spiritual experience and a psychic change. Isn't life going to be perfect from now on?

But this is the great test of the spiritual life. Am I going to keep doing this work even though it doesn't give me some spiritual buzz anymore, even though I feel mundane and human and sometimes even depressed? The mistake was that I had become attached to feeling good even in sobriety. I used tools solely meant to keep me sane in order to get high in sobriety. I couldn't or wouldn't do things that were good for me or for others just for the sake of doing them, just because they were the right things to do.

I began to realize that spirituality wasn't about trying to achieve constant rapture. Nope. Spirituality was about facing reality and being human. It was about feeling all facets of life, whether happy, sad, angry, lonely, good day, bad day, whatever day. So I pushed myself harder and refused to let feelings stop me. The inevitable result was that for the first time EVER, I evened out. It was the beginning of *real* strength. No more too high or too low. No more holes or cracks in my foundation. No longer just a flimsy shell. No longer insecure and ashamed of being a person. I stood with my feet on the ground. I could look life in the eye.

I came home one night after completing about half of my amends. As I sat down on the couch, something mystical occurred. A great sense of peace poured through me. It was another realized miracle and promise from the Big Book. A shower of relief soaked my spirit and I felt truly happy. Finally, I was okay. All worries and insecurities about my life vanished for good. To this day, I have been recovered. In fact, it just gets better and better.

11

SERVE

Nine months towards freedom when a $13,000 bill from the

IRS came in. I almost handed fear a free pass to once again saturate my

mind, but my gut told me not to give power to a ghost. I knew

everything would be all right. I prayed to God to help me stay away

from my old and apocalyptic mind, to put my feet on the ground, and

start moving.

I stared at the bill on my couch. It glared at me with its large

bold print. I hoped it might speak to me with some advice on how to

pay it. Frustrated, I got in my car and sped down to Staples to buy a

daily organizer. More frustrated, I sped over to the car wash to vacuum

the inside of my sedan until it was immaculate. That was my new way

of controlling my life. Cleaning, organizing, washing things spotless,

any kind of simple activity was capable of helping me deal with larger

issues. It's like laying out the ingredients before you make the

sandwich. So when the car and house were fit for a king, and any other possible chore or productive action exhausted, I found the strength to tackle my looming financial demon.

The IRS daunted me. Just calling a rep on the phone filled me with angst. But after sweating off my deodorant and conversing like an awkward teenager, I learned that there were three options: 1) pay it in full, 2) set up a payment plan, or 3) make a settlement offer that included an explanation. What was I to say?

"Listen, uh… I recently blew every last dime on heroin and purposely didn't pay taxes so how 'bout you guys just cut the bill by like, 75%, and we call it a day?"

In fact, that's pretty much what I said. Honesty was the only option. I spent weeks gathering copies of every bill, payment stub, loan and credit card balance, bank statement, medical receipt, everything… as well as my wife's entire financial situation, much to her dismay. I copied our entire lives and sent in the Offer in Compromise application with my insane explanation. $3,000 on $13,000 is a bit of a stretch. But guess what? They accepted my offer. And so I moved on to the loans, credit cards, and family.

Time to start working. A month or two of Charlie getting better was fine, but I was overdue. Reality changes. Failure to make amends with creditors would surely result in relapse, and eventually death. And yes, it is that important.

No job was too menial at this point. I applied everywhere and hoped to do service work, but for some reason I couldn't land jobs that I was overqualified for until I made my last amends. Maybe the Universe conspired to keep me from running myself into the ground until a solid foundation was laid. The day I made my final amends, #30 on the list, I got a job doing that which I had no experience whatsoever: cooking.

I showed up to an open house at an assisted living senior home and told them I had no cooking skills whatsoever. I was hired at $13 an hour. The call came in from the flamboyant kitchen manager. He needed a chef to fill hours and I needed a gig. He asked me why he should hire someone with the cooking prowess of a vending machine. All I could do was pour a bowl of cereal and boil pasta. I didn't go on and on bullshitting. I said only four things to him. "I'm honest, I work hard, I'll do what you tell me to do, and I can absorb a ton of information fast."

"Fine, I'll roll the dice with you, but if you can't hack it, we'll have to let you go."

Translation: If you suck, I fire you.

The kitchen was a circus. Eight hours passed and not a single thought entered my mind. I ran around like a madman, baking desert, making soup, preparing appetizers and entrees, and trying not to get burned by the steamer or lose one of my fingers in the meat slicer. I cooked single-handedly for 150 senior residents. It was satisfying to lay out an entire spread of food and deserts… and I know this is irrelevant, but my chicken noodle soup was delicious. Although, it probably wasn't too much of a shame that my patrons were all half-demented and forgot what they ate ten seconds after eating.

Every check that came in, I sent straight to Mom, Dad, Wife, and creditors. The rest went to food and rent. And so I chiseled away at the debt. Good things began happening at an increasingly frequent rate.

I soon finished a bachelor's degree I'd been working on for eleven years. It was the least I could do for my parents who'd spent hundreds of thousands of dollars trying to educate me properly. I graduated on the dean's list and received a diploma in psychology. No commencement ceremony was necessary for my 29 year-old undergraduate completion, considered bittersweet at this point. Wasting Mom and Dad's time was over. Withdrawing from semesters after refund deadlines had expired was over. Wasting opportunities that were laid at my feet to instead use drugs like a pig was over.

In the fall of 2006, I enrolled in a certificate program, an educational pre-requisite for obtaining the CADAC - Certified Alcohol & Drug Addiction Counselor. The program found me when UMASS Boston sent me a pamphlet advertising its new on-line version of their 'Alcohol/Chemical Dependency Treatment Services Program'. I figured I had to go do it, so I did. I soon discovered why.

On an unusually balmy November afternoon, I drove by my sponsor's ice cream shop, felt guilty for not stopping, and turned around to pull in. We sat outside on a bench and lit up a cigarette. Who should show up but a colorful group of teenage addicts and a staff member from an alternative high school geared for kids with addiction.

As they crossed the street and sauntered into the parking lot, the group appeared like a moving chimney. Smoke break for the kids. They introduced themselves at will and right away I knew what was coming.

"Listen guys, we need good people, sponsors, and people who know about addiction."

Enough said.

"You know what would be a great idea? Starting a Chapter 2 meeting for the kids."

I couldn't have imagined a better effort than letting teenagers know that they can get sober and not be completely miserable. Plus, the younger these guys recover, the more people they can go and help. Why spend millions of tax dollars on a recovery school and not give the students a solution? Moreover, why staff the place with public school educators as opposed to addiction specialists?

So I began volunteering to offer what I could. A month later, they asked me to jump on board full time to provide guidance, resources, and addictions education. But truthfully, I really just brought the exposure of a recovered person who had found a solution. I worked for the high school on my days off and cooked for the seniors the rest of the week. Within two months, I joined the school full time under a one-year contract.

I ended up working in several capacities; co-teaching and providing support in academic classes, adding structure to the daily schedule, educating staff, students, and families about addiction and the sort of efforts necessary to achieve lasting recovery and quality of life. I confronted students in relapse and tried to push them to make hard decisions. I asked them to consider doing some real work on themselves. I served as a traditional counselor by keeping records, providing case management, and making appropriate referrals to my friends up North. I set the kids up with sponsors and worked with them individually after school, on the weekends, at their houses, anywhere. I also tried to support family members and referred mothers to my sponsor, who set up a weekly mothers group. Finally, I led the Chapter 2 group for the students, illuminating the rigors behind the original Twelve Step process.

Eventually, it caught on. Kids were doing more than just barely staying sober, being handed free diplomas, and going on cushy vacations. I'm not sure rewarding selfish drug addicts whose mission in life is to manipulate everything and everyone to achieve greater personal comfort is the best strategy, but hey, what do I know? My theory is that if anyone should have to work for something, it is most certainly the easy-street drug addict. Unfortunately, that theory was not necessarily embraced by most of the staff.

Nonetheless, the teenage students were slowly changing. Some were even taking 3rd Steps and writing 4th Steps.

"Hey Charlie, guess what? I did the dishes for my mom last night. Isn't that good?"

"Yeah… it'd be even better if you didn't say anything about it."

"Charlie, look! I let the girl sit in the front seat. That's the right thing to do, right?"

"Yeah... but do it when I'm not around."

Others weren't so eager. Three times I drove to the house of a kid who I refused to give up on, walked straight through the door, dragged him out of bed, watched him pack his bags, and then hauled him off to detox. I didn't even care if he needed to get high on the way so long as he produced an ounce of willingness to get his ass up North. Other kids began the Step process, but weren't willing to continue once they realized there was some actual work to do.

"I can't write my inventory. I just don't have the time. These worldly clamors and distractions, I swear!"

Hmm... I wonder where he got that language?

"Time isn't the issue, kiddo. You don't want to do the work. You don't want to change. If you really wanted to finish your inventory, you'd lock yourself up in your room and not come out until you were either done, needed more paper, or started writing backwards."

Then there were the kids who just loved to argue.

"How am I being selfish if I'm only hurting myself?"

"Have you ever loved anybody?"

"Yeah, my mom."

"Wouldn't you be heartbroken if she started cutting herself or smoking crack?"

"Fine, but what if there was no one in my life and I lived alone on a mountain?"

"Well that's not the case, but even so, just being a human being demands you act in a way that you would recommend to all others. Where would our world be if we all acted the way you do?"

Just imagine an entire world of crackheads and drunks.

But my mission was to get just one kid get better. Miraculously, it turned out to be more than that. Some of them experienced new dimensions associated with an active spiritual life. Some saw the power of God working in their lives. Some I drove to department stores they'd stolen from to make amends. Let me tell you, seeing a drug-addicted teenager walk into a store they robbed and admit their wrong is truly something else. That single experience alone made it worthwhile.

Despite the seriousness with which I approach addiction and the spiritual life, understand that I'm still Charlie. I don't walk around cloaked in a satin robe with a long beard and dreadlocks, holding a staff and preaching the word of God to the heathen. I still swear, tease my friends, and have sex with my wife. I still have fun, play golf and tennis, watch movies, write music, and act in film and theatre. I go to the gym and run around. I work hard, but I also hang out with my family and friends. I do normal things and try to remain open-minded.

So I haven't castrated myself and joined the brethren in seclusion... but I was the guy tied to four-point restraints after being sectioned for drug-induced psychosis. I was the guy who lied every time he opened his mouth. I was the guy who manipulated you, betrayed you, hurt you, and stole from you. I was the guy who took your girlfriend or your wife and slept with her. I was the loud, obnoxious, selfish jerk everybody wants to get away from.

And I am also living proof that people can and do change.

IRS

Department of the Treasury
Internal Revenue Service

www.irs.gov

Form 656 (Rev. 7-2004)
Catalog Number 16728N

**Attach
Application
Fee (check or
money order)
here.**

Form 656

Offer in Compromise

IRS RECEIVED DATE

RECEIVED IRS
19
MAY 11 2006
419
IRS

M A I L

Item 1 — Taxpayer's Name and Home or Business Street Address

Charles Augustus Peabody

Name

Name

Street Address

City   State   ZIP Code

Mailing Address (if different from above)

Street Address

City   State   ZIP Code

DATE RETURNED

Item 2 — Social Security Numbers

(a) Primary ▮▮▮▮▮▮▮▮

(b) Secondary _____

Item 3 — Employer Identification Number (included in offer)

_____

Item 4 — Other Employer Identification Numbers (not included in offer) _____

_____

Item 5 — To: Commissioner of Internal Revenue Service

I/We (includes all types of taxpayers) submit this offer to compromise the tax liabilities plus any interest, penalties, additions to tax, and additional amounts required by law (tax liability) for the tax type and period marked below: (Please mark an "X" in the box for the correct description and fill-in the correct tax period(s), adding additional periods if needed).

☒ 1040/1120 Income Tax — Year(s) 2004 + 2005

☐ 941 Employer's Quarterly Federal Tax Return — Quarterly period(s) _____

_____

☐ 940 Employer's Annual Federal Unemployment (FUTA) Tax Return — Year(s) _____

☐ Trust Fund Recovery Penalty as a responsible person of (enter corporation name) _____

_____

for failure to pay withholding and Federal Insurance Contributions Act Taxes (Social Security taxes), for period(s) ending _____

☐ Other Federal Tax(es) [specify type(s) and period(s)] _____

Note: If you need more space, use another sheet entitled "Attachment to Form 656 Dated _____." Sign and date the attachment following the listing of the tax periods.

Item 6 — I/We submit this offer for the reason(s) checked below:

☐ **Doubt as to Liability** — "I do not believe I owe this tax." You must include a detailed explanation of the reason(s) why you believe you do not owe the tax in Item 9.

☒ **Doubt as to Collectibility** — "I have insufficient assets and income to pay the full amount." You must include a complete Collection Information Statement, Form 433-A and/or Form 433-B.

☐ **Effective Tax Administration** — "I owe this amount and have sufficient assets to pay the full amount, but due to my exceptional circumstances, requiring full payment would cause an economic hardship or would be unfair and inequitable." You must include a complete Collection Information Statement, Form 433-A and/or Form 433B and complete Item 9.

Item 7

I/We offer to pay $ 3,000 (must be more than zero). Complete item 10 to explain where you will obtain the funds to make this offer.

Check only one of the following:

☒ **Cash Offer** (Offered amount will be paid in 90 days or less.)

Balance to be paid in: ☐ 10, ☒ 30, ☐ 60, or ☐ 90 days from written notice of acceptance of the offer.

☐ **Short-Term Deferred Payment Offer** (Offered amount paid in MORE than 90 days but within 24 months from written notice of acceptance of the offer.)

$_____ within _____ days (not more than 90 — See Instructions Section, **Determine Your Payment Terms**) from written notice of acceptance of the offer; and/or

beginning in the _____ month after written notice of acceptance of the offer $_____ on the _____ day of each month for a total of _____ months. (Cannot extend more than 24 months from written notice of acceptance of the offer.)

☐ **Deferred Payment Offer** (Offered amount will be paid over the remaining life of the collection statute.)

$_____ within _____ days (not more than 90 — See Instructions Section, **Determine Your Payment Terms**) from written notice of acceptance of the offer; and

beginning in the first month after written notice of acceptance of the offer $_____ on the _____ day of each month for a total of _____ months.

Item 9 — Explanation of Circumstances

I am requesting an offer in compromise for the reason(s) listed below:

Note: If you are requesting compromise based on doubt as to liability, explain why you don't believe you owe the tax.
If you believe you have special circumstances affecting your ability to fully pay the amount due, explain your situation. You may attach additional sheets if necessary. Please include your name and SSN or EIN on all additional sheets or supporting documentation.

After making selfish and irresponsible choices fueled by my alcohol and drug addiction in 2004 and 2005, I went to treatment in Plymouth N.H. July 05 and have been recovering, making ammends, running AA Meetings, an trying to grow up and put my life back together in a mature and accountable way. I full responsibility for these taxes however, I have been unemployed for the past nine mo. in an effort to become a sane & better person. I am broke, have thousands of other debt, have

Item 10 — Source of Funds

I/We shall obtain the funds to make this offer from the following source(s): assets, and am unable to pay this liability. However, my family is will to help me to the extent they can, and I feel this would be the only timely mann. to resolve this for both of interests.

My father, Charles A. Peabody, Through his financial representative ▇▇▇▇▇▇▇▇ Esq. (note: My father is unable to allocate funds directly because he is in late Dementia

Item 11 — Mandatory Signature(s)

If I/We submit this offer on a substitute form, I/we affirm that this form is a verbatim duplicate of the official Form 656, and I/we agree to be bound by all the terms and conditions set forth in the official Form 656.

Under penalties of perjury, I declare that I have examined this offer, including accompanying schedules and statements, and to the best of my knowledge and belief, it is true, correct and complete

11(a) Signature of Taxpayer *Charles A. Peabody*

Date 05/06/06

11(b) Signature of Taxpayer

Date

For Official Use Only

I accept the waiver of the statutory period limitations on assessment for the Internal Revenue Service, as d▇▇▇d in Item 8(e).

Signature of Authorized Internal Revenue Service Official

Title *Process Examiner*

Date 5-12-06 - P

Item 12 — If this application was prepared by someone other than the tapayer, please fill in that person's name and address below.

Name: _____

Address: _____
(if known)

Item 13 Paid Preparer's Use Only	Preparer's signature ▶		Date	Check if self-employed ☐	Preparer's CAF no. or PTIN
	Firm's name (or yours if self-employed), address, and ZIP code ▶			EIN	
				Phone no. ( )	

Item 14 Third Party Designee	Do you want to allow another person to discuss this offer with the IRS?		☐ Yes. Complete the following.		☐ No
	Designee's name ▶		Phone no. ▶ ( )		

Department of the Treasury

Internal Revenue Service
Centralized OIC
███████████████

CHARLES AUGUSTUS PEABODY
███████████████

Date of this Letter:

Person to Contact: JUN 1 9 2006

Employee #: ████████
Phone#: ████████

Taxpayer ID#: ████████
Offer Number: ████████

Dear Mr. Peabody,

We have accepted your offer in compromise signed and dated by you on 05/06/2006. The date of acceptance is the date of this letter and our acceptance is subject to the terms and conditions on the enclosed Form 656, Offer in Compromise.

Please note that the conditions of the offer require you to file and pay all required taxes for five tax years or the period of time payments are being made on the offer, whichever is longer. This will begin on the date shown in the upper right hand corner of this letter.

Additionally, please remember that the conditions of the offer include the provision that as additional consideration for the offer, we will retain any refunds or credits that you may be entitled to receive for 2006 or for earlier tax years. This includes refunds you receive in 2007 for any overpayments you made toward tax year 2006 or toward earlier tax years. The Notice of Federal Tax Lien will be released when the offer amount is paid in full.

If you are required to make any payments under this agreement, make your check or money order payable to the United States Treasury and send it to:
Internal Revenue Service

Please send all other correspondence to:
Internal Revenue Service

You must promptly notify the Internal Revenue Service of any change in your address or marital status. This will ensure we have the proper address to advise you of the status of your offer.

continued on next page

12

RECOVERED.

For me, it has been over five years since I walked into detox a trembling, emaciated wreck and into the hands of God up North. I left the detox unit gaunt, discolored, dope sick, deranged, hopeless, and with no real intention of actually giving up drugs and alcohol for the rest of my life. I didn't think it was possible for someone in my condition to get better and stay better. I figured I was doomed to die a useless heroin addict. But instead, I've done more in these last five years than in the entire preceding 28 years of my life.

Since taking Steps up North and returning to our world, I have made amends to over thirty people, including old friends, enemies, bosses, relatives, in-laws, stores, banks, and the big bad IRS. I have erased over $30,000 of debt, paid in full. I have graduated from college on the dean's list. I have completed a certificate program in addictions counseling and have two thousand clinical work hours towards becoming licensed by the state and certified nationally. I have become a teacher in the state of Massachusetts for health, family, and consumer sciences. I have passed the GRE with flying colors and am prepared to embark on a possible Masters degree program. I can work a 40-hour week happily, without having to be high as hell all day long. And I have begun writing, playing music, and acting again… on stage as opposed to off.

More importantly, I have repaired broken and lost relationships. I have rebuilt bridges once burned. I have worked with numbers of addicts, families, and spouses of addicts. I have led groups, spoke publically, and started forums that bring a spiritual solution to others. All of my free time goes to my wife and family, who I love being with now. My wife and I have grown together in unimaginable ways and live a comfortable, content life together. Even she has taken Steps and changed. More miraculous is that people trust me, turn to me, and count on me.

Nothing is wrong anymore and I haven't a single regret. I'm happy, strong, and at peace. I've learned to be content with less. I can sit down and feel calm inside without the TV on, music going, phone dialing, or any other distraction I was once dependant on. I can fall asleep at night and rest soundly. I quit smoking after a pack a day for 17 years, telling myself that nicotine was just another wall between me and God. I take care of myself by eating healthy and exercising regularly. I floss and brush everyday. I even go to the dentist twice a year.

I haven't had a single thought or desire to drink or get high since choosing to get better at some point during treatment up North. I can purposely think about cold beers, kind bud, OxyContin, or heroin and those thoughts have no power over me. I have lived through three recent deaths in my family, including the death of my father, without the slightest urge to self-destruct. I underwent the knife twice, once for abdominal surgery and once for wrist surgery, and refused narcotics of any sort. Sure it hurt like hell, but it wasn't impossible. I'm not willing to lose what I have now. I want to grow.

So I am a free man and can go anywhere on earth safely. I am completely un-medicated and have been since detox. I no longer suffer from mild depression, major depression, bipolar disorder, or depression not otherwise specified. I no longer suffer from anxiety disorders or personality disorders, nor do I require any sort of psychotropic medication to be okay. I have raised my serotonin levels back to normal through consistent prayer, meditation, and right action alone. Any one of the many sane people around me will attest that I have never been more grounded, healthy, or responsible in my life. And if I do get stuck,

I slow down, stay out of the past or the future, and just do what's right in front of me. One step at a time.

Moral, spiritual action alone has gotten me better. And God is solely responsible for this. Life experience is fundamentally different, as if something in my mind has cracked wide open. My once shrinking world has suddenly begun expanding. It is a new dimension and I am constantly in it. The dark, empty, sad hole that followed me around has been filled up with Light. I walk around now and feel lifted up for no reason at all. Best of all, I have control over my thoughts, words, emotions, and actions. I have the power of choice back. I have changed. I am recovered.

So to dispel the false cliché and myth that people *don't* change:

People *Do* Change.

I am living proof of it. Thank you for reading my story.

EPILOGUE

I have since moved on from the alternative high school and have begun other work and projects that I feel I must complete. My hope is to raise or make enough money to open up a local treatment center in Massachusetts, similar to the one up North, in order to help the many addicts who suffer right here at home. Eventually, it is my hope that many others will open more treatment centers dedicated to the spiritual principles of the Twelve Steps and to other lifestyle changes in the areas of nutrition, movement therapy, meditation, alternative medicine, and other approaches conducive to mental, physical, and spiritual health. Furthermore, I hope that the truth about addiction and recovery will infiltrate mainstream thinking and attitudes, thereby changing ineffective conventional treatments. Finally, my hope is that the CRUCIAL SPIRITUAL COMPONENT to recovery will not be ignored anymore and will become an integral part of all state and federally funded substance abuse programs.

*

Thank you to all of my friends and family. Thank you to my beautiful wife, Isabelle. Thank you to my Mom, Dorothy. Thank you to my sister, Abby. Thank you to all of my guides and teachers. Thank you to the staff up North. Thank you God. I am still and I know.

REFERENCES

Alcoholics Anonymous World Services, Inc. Alcoholics Anonymous –

Fourth Edition. New York City, 2001.

ABOUT THE AUTHOR

Charlie Peabody is an actor, writer, musician, and investor. He holds a degree in Psychology from UMASS Boston. He is a certified MA teacher for health sciences. He is a sponsor/addictions counselor and is currently CADAC eligible, after completing UMASS Boston's Alcohol/Chemical Dependency Treatment Services Program. Charlie is also a licensed real estate agent and currently owns and manages residential property in Massachusetts. Finally, Charlie continues his creative passion for theatre, film, writing and music. He is currently working on a new fiction novel as well as a compilation of comedy sketches. He lives with his wife, son and dog in New England.

www.charliepeabody.com